PENGUIN BOOKS

Steve Jackson's Sorcery!
THE SHAMUTANTI HILLS

Steve Jackson is an internationally known figure in the fantasy-games world. He is cofounder of Games Workshop Ltd., the largest British company specializing in such games. Its activities include publishing *White Dwarf*, a magazine devoted to science fiction and fantasy games, and organizing Britain's largest games convention, Games Day, which is held in London every September.

Mr. Jackson attended Altrincham School in Cheshire and went on to the University of Keele, where he studied biology and psychology; while at college, he founded the university's games society. After writing on a free-lance basis for the professional games magazine *Games & Puzzles*, he coauthored, with Ian Livingstone, *The Warlock of Firetop Mountain*, a fantasy book for children. He was the sole author of two other books in the same series, *The Citadel of Chaos* and *Spaceship Traveler*.

In addition to *The Shamutanti Hills*, the *Sorcery!* series comprises *The Spell Book* (also available from Penguin Books) as well as *Kharé—Cityport of Traps*, *The Seven Serpents*, and *The Crown of Kings* (all to be published by Penguin).

THE
SHAMUTANTI
HILLS

PENGUIN BOOKS

To Ian Livingstone

Penguin Books Ltd, Harmondsworth,
Middlesex, England
Penguin Books, 40 West 23rd Street,
New York, New York 10010, U.S.A.
Penguin Books Australia Ltd, Ringwood,
Victoria, Australia
Penguin Books Canada Limited, 2801 John Street,
Markham, Ontario, Canada L3R 1B4
Penguin Books (N.Z.) Ltd, 182–190 Wairau Road,
Auckland 10, New Zealand

First published in Great Britain by
Penguin Books 1983
First published in the United States of America by
Penguin Books 1984

Copyright © Steve Jackson, 1983
Illustrations copyright © John Blanche, 1983
All rights reserved

Library of Congress Catalog Card Number: 84-60574

Printed in the United States of America by
R.R. Donnelley & Sons Company, Harrisonburg, Virginia
Set in Palatino

Except in the United States of America,
this book is sold subject to the condition
that it shall not, by way of trade or otherwise,
be lent, re-sold, hired out, or otherwise circulated
without the publisher's prior consent in any form of
binding or cover other than that in which it is
published and without a similar condition
including this condition being imposed
on the subsequent purchaser

CONTENTS

INTRODUCTION

You are about to embark on an epic adventure – a quest for the Crown of Kings. Your journey will take you from Analand, your home, across the unruly territories of Kakhabad to the Mampang Fortress wherein lies the treasured crown.

In this solo fantasy role-playing gamebook you may elect to become either a wizard or a warrior. If you choose to be a warrior, a simple combat system will allow you to fight the various creatures of Kakhabad quickly and conveniently. If you choose wizardry as your skill, you will learn to master a unique magic system found in no other fantasy role-playing game. As would a real Grand Wizard, you will have to *learn* your spells!

The spells available to you are found in the *Spell Book*, which is published separately, and you will prepare for your journey by memorizing these spells. you need not learn *all* the spells, for all forty-eight spells would be known only by a true Imperial Sorcerer. A basic knowledge of as few as six spells will be enough for you to start your journey.

Whether wizard or warrior, the journey ahead will be dangerous and you will be faced with tricks, traps, problems and clues – not to mention the host of evil creatures which will try to prevent you reaching your goal.

Through the multi-choice gamebook system, *you* will choose which paths to take, whether to fight or flee from combat and how you will solve problems. If death takes you, you will have to begin your adventure again. But if your skill is great and if luck – and your god – is with you, you may survive your overland journey to the Mampang Fortress.

THE SIMPLE AND ADVANCED GAMES

Beginners may wish to start with the simple game, ignoring the use of magic. Rules for fighting creatures with swords and other weapons are given in each adventure book, using a combat system similar to that used in Puffin's *The Warlock of Firetop Mountain*, the original Fighting Fantasy Gamebook. By rolling dice, you battle creatures with weapons only.

More experienced players will wish to progress quickly on to the advanced game, in which your fighting ability is somewhat limited but your most powerful weapon will be your knowledge of magic, a much more powerful tool. In actual fact, the advanced game is fairly simple to learn. There is no reason why beginners should not proceed with the use of magic from the start. But learning spells will take some time and practice with the Spell Book, and the 'simple' option is given for players who wish to start their adventure with minimum delay.

HOW TO FIGHT THE CREATURES OF KAKHABAD

Before setting off on your journey, you must first build up your own personality profile. On pages 18 and 19 you will find an *Adventure Sheet*. This is a sort of 'current status report' which will help you keep track of your adventure. Your own SKILL, STAMINA and LUCK scores will be recorded here, and also the equipment, artefacts and treasures you will find on your journey. Since the details will change constantly, you are advised to take photocopies of the blank *Adventure Sheet* to use in future adventures, or write in pencil so that the previous adventure can be erased when you start another.

Skill, Stamina and Luck

Roll one die. If you are playing as a *warrior* (the simple game), add 6 to this number and enter the total in the SKILL box on your *Adventure Sheet*. If you are playing as a *wizard* (the advanced game), add only 4 to this number and enter the total. Wizards are worse fighters than warriors, but they more than make up for this by the use of magic spells.

Roll both dice. Add 12 to the number rolled and enter this total in the STAMINA box.

There is also a LUCK box. Roll one die, add 6 to this number and enter this total in the LUCK box.

For reasons that will be explained below, SKILL, STAMINA and LUCK scores change constantly during an adventure. You must keep an accurate record of these scores and for this reason you are advised either to write small in the boxes or to keep an eraser handy. But never rub out your *Initial* scores. Although you may be awarded additional SKILL, STAMINA and LUCK points, these totals may never exceed your *Initial* scores, except on very rare occasions, when you will be instructed on a particular page.

Your SKILL score reflects your swordsmanship and general fighting expertise; the higher the better. Your STAMINA score reflects your general constitution, your will to survive, your determination and overall fitness; the higher your STAMINA score, the longer you will be able to survive. Your LUCK score indicates how naturally lucky a person you are. Luck – and magic – are facts of life in the fantasy world you are about to explore.

Battles

You will often come across pages in the book which instruct you to fight a creature of some sort. An option to flee may be given, but if not – or if you choose to attack the creature anyway – you must resolve the battle as described below.

First record the creature's SKILL and STAMINA scores in the first vacant Monster Encounter Box on your *Adventure Sheet*. The scores for each creature are given in the book each time you have an encounter. The sequence of combat is then:

1. Roll the two dice once for the creature. Add its SKILL score. This total is the creature's Attack Strength.
2. Roll the two dice once for yourself. Add the number rolled to your current SKILL score. This total is your Attack Strength.
3. If your Attack Strength is higher than that of the creature, you have wounded it. Proceed to step 4. If the creature's Attack Strength is higher than yours, it has wounded you. Proceed to step 5. If both Attack Strength totals are the same, you have avoided each other's blows – start the next Attack Round from step 1 above.
4. You have wounded the creature, so subtract 2 points from its STAMINA score. You may use your LUCK here to do additional damage (see over).
5. The creature has wounded you, so subtract 2 points from your STAMINA score. Again, you may use LUCK at this stage (see over).
6. Make the appropriate adjustments to either the creature's or your own STAMINA score (and your LUCK score if you used LUCK – see over).
7. Begin the next Attack Round (repeat steps 1–6). This sequence continues until the STAMINA score of either you or the creature you are fighting has been reduced to zero (death).

Fighting More Than One Creature

If you come across more than one creature in a particular encounter, the instructions on that page will tell you how to handle the battle. Sometimes you will treat them as a single monster; sometimes you will fight each one in turn.

Luck

At various times during your adventure, either in battles or when you come across situations in which you could be either lucky or unlucky (details of these are given on the pages themselves), you may call on your LUCK to make the outcome more favourable. But beware! Using LUCK is a risky business and if you are *un*lucky, the results could be disastrous.

The procedure for using your LUCK is as follows: roll two dice. If the number rolled is *equal to or less than* your current LUCK score, you have been *Lucky* and the result will go in your favour. If the number rolled is *higher* than your current LUCK score, you have been *Unlucky* and you will be penalized.

This procedure is known as *Testing your Luck*. Each time you *Test your Luck*, you must subtract one point from your current LUCK score. Thus you will soon realize that the more you rely on your LUCK, the more risky this will become.

Using Luck in Battles

On certain pages of the book you will be told to *Test your Luck* and will be told the consequences of your being *Lucky* or *Unlucky*. However, in battles you always have the *option* of using your LUCK either to inflict a more serious wound on a creature you have just wounded, or to minimize the effects of a wound the creature has just inflicted on you.

If you have just wounded the creature, you may *Test your Luck* as described above. If you are *Lucky*, you have inflicted a severe wound and may subtract an *extra* 2 points from the creature's STAMINA score. However, if you are *Unlucky*, the wound was a mere graze and you must restore 1 point to the creature's STAMINA (i.e. instead of scoring the normal 2 points of damage, you have now scored only 1).

If the creature has just wounded you, you may *Test your Luck* to try to minimize the wound. If you are *Lucky*, you have managed to avoid the full damage of the blow. Restore 1 point of STAMINA (i.e. instead of doing 2 points of damage it has done only 1). If you are *Unlucky*, you have taken a more serious blow. Subtract 1 *extra* STAMINA point.

Remember that you must subtract 1 point from your own LUCK score each time you *Test your Luck*.

Restoring Skill, Stamina and Luck

Skill

Your SKILL score will not change much during your adventure. Occasionally, you may be given instructions to increase or decrease your SKILL score. A Magic Weapon may increase your SKILL, but remember that only one weapon can be used at a time! You cannot claim 2 SKILL bonuses for carrying two Magic Swords. Your SKILL score can never exceed its *Initial* value unless specifically instructed.

Stamina and Provisions

Your STAMINA score will change a lot during your adventure as you fight monsters and undertake arduous tasks. As you near your goal, your STAMINA level may be dangerously low and battles may be particularly risky, so be careful!

You start with enough Provisions for two meals. You may rest and eat only when allowed by the instructions, and you may eat only one meal at a time. When you eat a meal, add points to your STAMINA score as instructed. Remember that you have a long way to go, so manage your Provisions wisely!

Remember also that your STAMINA score may never exceed its *Initial* value unless specifically instructed.

Luck

Additions to your LUCK score are awarded through the adventure when you have been particularly lucky. Details are given whenever this occurs. Remember that, as with SKILL and STAMINA, your LUCK score may never exceed its *Initial* value unless specifically instructed.

SKILL, STAMINA and LUCK scores can be restored to their *Initial* values by calling on your goddess (see later).

ALTERNATIVE DICE

If you do not have a pair of dice handy, dice rolls are printed
throughout the book at the bottom of the pages. Flicking rapidly
through the book and stopping on a page will give you a random dice
roll. If you need to 'roll' only one die, read only the first printed die; if
two, total the two dice symbols.

WIZARDS:
HOW TO USE MAGIC

If you have chosen to become a wizard you will have the option, throughout the adventure, of using magic spells. All the spells known to the sorcerers of Analand are listed in a separate volume, *The Sorcery! Spell Book*, and you will need to study this before you set off on your adventure.

All spells are coded with a three-letter code and you must learn and practise your spells until you are able to identify a reasonable number of them from their codes. Casting a spell drains your STAMINA and each has a cost, in STAMINA points, for its use. Recommended basic spells will get you started quickly, but are very uneconomical; an experienced wizard will use these only if faced with choices of unknown spells or if he/she has not found the artefact required for a less costly spell.

Full rules for using spells are given in the *Spell Book*.

DON'T FORGET! You may not refer to the SPELL BOOK once you have started your adventure.

LIBRA –
THE GODDESS OF JUSTICE

During your adventure you will be watched over by your own goddess, Libra. If the going gets tough, you may call on her for aid. *But she will only help you once in each adventure.* Once you have called on her help in the Shamutanti Hills, she will not listen to you again until you reach Kharé.

There are three ways in which she may help you:

Revitalization: You may call on her at any time to restore your SKILL, STAMINA and LUCK scores to their *Initial* values. This is not given as an option in the text; you may do this if and when you wish, but only once in each adventure.

Escape: Occasionally, when you are in danger, the text will offer you the option of calling on Libra to help you.

Removal of Curses and Diseases: She will remove any curses or diseases you may pick up on your adventure. This is not given as an option in the text; you may do this if and when you wish, but only once in each adventure.

EQUIPMENT
AND PROVISIONS

You start your adventure with the bare necessities of life. You have a sword as your weapon, and a backpack to hold your equipment, treasures, artefacts and provisions. You cannot take your *Spell Book* with you, as the sorcerers of Analand cannot risk its falling into the wrong hands in Kakhabad – so you may not refer to this book at all once you have started your journey.

You have a pouch around your waist containing 20 Gold Pieces, the universal currency of all the known lands. You will need money for food, shelter, purchases and bribery throughout your adventure, and 20 Gold Pieces will not go far. You will find it necessary to collect more gold as you progress on your way.

You are also carrying Provisions (food and drink) sufficient for 2 meals only. As you will find, food is an important commodity and you will have to be careful how you use it. Make sure you do not waste food: you cannot afford to run out of Provisions.

SORCERY! ADVENTURE SHEET

SKILL
Initial
Skill=

STAMINA
Initial
Stamina=

LUCK
Initial
Luck=

GOLD AND TREASURE

PROVISIONS

EQUIPMENT AND ARTEFACTS

BONUSES, PENALTIES, CURSES ETC.

CLUES AND NOTES

MONSTER ENCOUNTER BOXES

Skill=
Stamina=

Skill=
Stamina=

Skill=
Stamina=

Skill=
Stamina=

Skill=
Stamina=

Skill=
Stamina=

Skill=
Stamina=

Skill=
Stamina=

Skill=
Stamina=

Skill=
Stamina=

Skill=
Stamina=

Skill=
Stamina=

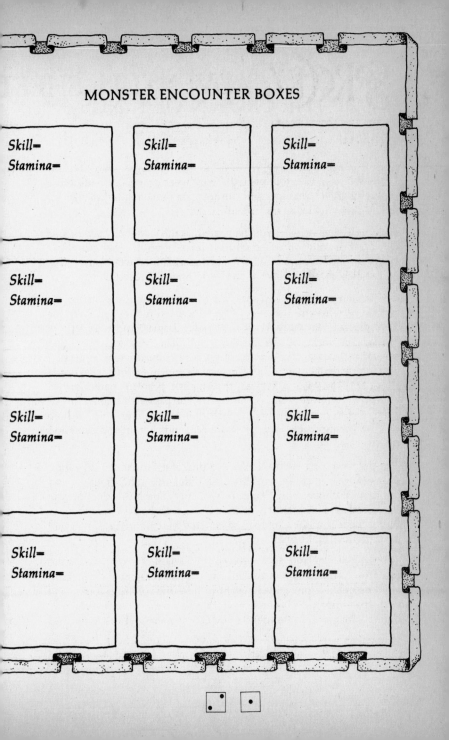

THE LEGEND
OF THE CROWN OF KINGS

Centuries ago, in the time we now call the Dark Ages, whole regions of the world were undiscovered. There were pockets of civilization, each with their own races and cultures. One such region was Kakhabad, a dark land at the end of the earth.

Although several warlords had tried, Kakhabad had never been ruled. All manner of evil creatures, forced from the more civilized lands beyond the Zanzunu Peaks, had gradually crawled into Kakhabad, which became known as the Verminpit at Earth End.

Civilization and order had spread throughout the rest of the known world ever since the discovery of the Crown of Kings by Chalanna the Reformer, of Femphrey. With its help, Chalanna became Emperor of the largest empire in the eastern world. This magical Crown had mysterious powers, bestowing supernormal qualities of leadership and justice on its owner. But Chalanna's own ambitions were not of conquest. He wished instead to establish peaceful nation-states, aligned to Femphrey. Thus in his wisdom he passed the fabled Crown from ruler to ruler in the neighbouring kingdoms, and, with the help of its magical powers, one by one these lands became peaceful and prosperous.

The path was set. Each ruler would own the Crown of Kings for a four-year period in which to establish order within his kingdom and fall in with the growing Femphrey Alliance. So far the kingdoms of Ruddlestone, Lendleland, Gallantaria and Brice had taken their turns under the rule of the Crown. The benefits were immediate. War and strife were virtually unknown.

The King of Analand duly received the Crown of Kings amid great ceremony, and, from that day onwards, the development of Analand was ensured. No one quite knew how the Crown of Kings could have such an enormous uplifting effect on a whole nation. Some said it was divinely inspired; some that its power was merely in the mind. But one thing was certain – its effects were unquestionable. All was well in Analand, until the night of the Black Moon.

The King was the first to discover that the Crown was missing. Carried off on that starless night by Birdmen from Xamen, the Crown was on its way to Mampang in the outlaw territories of Kakhabad. News came from the Baklands that the Crown was being carried to the Archmage of Mampang whose ambitions were to make Kakhabad his kingdom.

Although Kakhabad was a dangerous land, it was in itself little threat to the surrounding kingdoms. The lack of rule meant it had no army and its own internal struggles kept it permanently preoccupied. But with the Crown of Kings to establish rule, Kakhabad could potentially be a deadly enemy to all members of the Femphrey Alliance.

Such was the shame that fell on Analand for the loss of the Crown that all benefits from two years under its rule soon disappeared. Law, order and morale were breaking down. The King was losing the confidence of his subjects. Neighbouring territories were looking suspiciously across their borders. There were even whisperings of invasions.

One hope remained. Someone – for a military force would never survive the journey – must travel to Mampang and rescue the Crown of Kings. Only on its safe return would the dreadful curse be lifted from Analand. You have volunteered yourself for this quest and your mission is clear. You must cross Kakhabad to the Mampang Fortress and find the Crown!

KAKHABAD

ILKLAR.

TIN PANG R.

THE ZANZUNU PEAKS

L. ILKLALA

VISCHLAMI R.

MAMPANG
FORTRESS

VISCHLAMI
SWAMP

HIGH
XAMEN

LOW
XAMEN

FOREST OF THE SNATTA

AVANTI
WOOD

KHARABAK R.

NACOMANTI R.

YADU

COASTLINE

BAD SEA

You awake at sunrise. After dressing, you breakfast on bread and goat's milk and collect your belongings. Outside, the Outpost Settlement is stirring: the womenfolk emerge to wash and prepare their meals as the day's guard takes over.

Eyes follow you as you leave your hut and walk towards the Shamutanti Wall. The frontierspeople are well aware of your mission and a small crowd of well-wishers follows some distance behind you.

Before you stands the Cantopani Gate. Guarded constantly by Sightmaster Warriors, chosen for their powers of telescopic vision, the Gate is the final doorway between Analand and Kakhabad. Once more you check your pack.

Satisfied that your preparations are complete, you nod to the Sightmaster Sergeant. For the last time he glances at the look-out atop the gate, who signals the all-clear. The Sergeant orders the bolt to be withdrawn. A doorway opens up in front of you and you get your first view of the Shamutanti foothills, the first stage of your journey.

The Sightmaster Sergeant strides over and grasps your hand. 'I will not wish you a safe journey, for the way ahead will not be safe. Kakhabad is a treacherous land inhabited by devils. But this you already know.

'Take the path ahead to Cantopani, a small settlement of traders – although most are rogues and thieves – which you should reach within the hour. From Cantopani onwards there are three routes through Birritanti to Kharé, a cityport on the Jabaji river. From Kharé you must cross the Baklands, which are unknown. It is said that day and night in the Baklands are controlled not by the sun but by supernatural forces; and bear in mind also that, from Kharé onwards, your progress will be *watched*.'

His warnings do little to inspire confidence in you. He continues: 'But I have observed your training and you are indeed a worthy champion. I wish you luck and success with your quest. My thoughts, and the good wishes of all the peoples of Analand, will be with you. With Libra on your side may you live to lift the curse and depression which rack our kingdom.'

You shake his hand, thank him for his good wishes and step up to the

Gate. Resolutely, you pass through the doorway. The faces of the folk watching your departure reveal the hopes that rest with you and with the success of your quest.

With a wave, you turn and face the hills. The early morning air is crisp and the rising sun paints the hills in colours of natural beauty which conceal the devilry ahead.

Setting off determinedly, you follow the path. Your quest has begun! Turn to **178**.

2

As you draw your weapon, you hear a hissing noise and the body of a huge, two-tailed SERPENT materializes before your eyes. One of its tails is wrapped around your arm and now, with a flick, the creature sends you flying into the undergrowth. Lose 1 STAMINA point. You pick yourself up and face the creature. Resolve your combat:

SERPENT   SKILL 7   STAMINA 8

If you win, you may continue through the bush until you reach a point where the undergrowth thins and becomes a waist-high grass-land. Turn to **105**.

3

Following the passage down for some distance, you reach a T-junction where you may turn left (turn to **63**) or right (turn to **26**).

4

The cage door is firmly locked. If you have a key with you, you may try using it on the door by subtracting 10 from the number on the key and turning to that reference, or you may try a spell:

GOP	DOP	BAM	PEP	RAZ
443	409	320	429	360

Alternatively, you may try breaking the lock (turn to **142**).

5

You ask what sort of teeth the bag contains, but he will only tell you 'creature teeth' and he certainly will not trust you to look through the bag. He will charge you 3 Gold Pieces for the bag of teeth. Buy if you will, then turn to **280**.

6

As you tread carefully along the passage, dust falls from the low ceiling. Precarious wooden beams hold the walls back and you stumble and curse as your foot strikes one of the beams. Suddenly a pile of rubble falls from the ceiling in front of you and a cracking of wood stops you cold. The roof is collapsing! Will you turn and run back to the door (turn to **66**) or run on ahead (turn to **128**) to avoid the falling rocks?

7

Running ahead quickly, you are eventually out of range of the annoying little creatures. You follow the path for the rest of the afternoon until you reach a point where you can see that it is running into a hill village. Proceed by turning to **28**.

8

You settle down and relax on the bed. Outside the inn there is a commotion and you spring up as several Svinns burst into your room and surround you. Before you can react, two grasp your hands and you are marched from the inn to a hut at the edge of the village. Turn to **71**.

9

You may continue your journey either by following the path into the valley (turn to **164**) or by taking the high path up into the hills (turn to **157**).

10

Eventually the path peters out and ahead of you is a wood. A signpost, reading TO ALIANNA, points into the wood. Will you set off into the woods (turn to **150**) or return to the junction and continue heading northwards as you were before (turn to **46**)?

11

You pull out your bamboo pipe and begin to play. Somehow the unseen musicians adapt their tune to accommodate you and play away merrily for half an hour or so. You may add 3 STAMINA points and 1 LUCK point for your restful encounter. Then you pick yourself up, leave the hut and make your way out of the village. Turn to **196**.

12

As they see you, they all point and gabble excitedly to one another. One of them rises into the air and flies across, hovering over you to take a closer look. Will you attempt to speak with him (turn to **113**) or will you hold your ground and prepare to take defensive action (turn to **203**)?

13

You follow a path leading sharply downhill into a narrow valley. You cross a stream on a wooden bridge and start to climb the next hill. Half-way up, you hear twigs break in the undergrowth and suddenly a large creature – about the size of a bear – stands before you. It has black and white fur, and a long bushy tail which trails out behind it. This animal bars your way and is snarling menacingly at you. Will you prepare to attack it (turn to **252**) or try to edge round it peacefully (turn to **236**)?

14

Outside the village you climb up into the woods. You find a suitable sheltered spot not far from another path. Will you camp for the night (turn to **108**) or continue through the night (turn to **49**)?

15

As the dying Ogre is heaving its last breath, you investigate the room. You try grinding some of the black rock as the creature was doing but you cannot turn the handle. However, two valuable gems have already been processed and are lying on the table. You may take these with you. Each is worth 10 Gold Pieces but if you wish to buy anything with them, you will not be given change. In other words, it will cost you a whole gem to buy an item costing, for instance, only 2 Gold Pieces. You may now leave the room and the cave, and return to the junction (turn to **144**).

16

The passage slopes downhill and you soon reach a fork where you may go either right (turn to **174**) or left (turn to **151**).

17

'In this wood I have collected all sorts of magical artefacts,' she says. 'Release me from this cage and I will give you three useful items.' Will you try to free her (turn to 4) or search for the items anyway (turn to 213)?

18

You sit down and eat and admire the fine view of the surrounding hillside. If this is your first meal today, add 2 STAMINA points. If you have already eaten since leaving Analand, add only 1 STAMINA point. When you are ready to continue, turn to 168.

19

The path winds up and over the hill and you stop and marvel at a grassy verge in which are growing some of the most beautiful and delicate flowers you have ever seen. Turn to 40.

20

The creature is a SKUNKBEAR and, when you draw your weapon, it raises its tail, releasing a nauseating odour. The smell is horrendous, but you must fight:

SKUNKBEAR   SKILL 7   STAMINA 5

The effect of the smell is so powerful that you must deduct 2 points from your dice roll each time you roll for Attack Strength. If you beat the creature, turn to 193.

21

You find a quiet place to rest outside the village. Away from the bustle of the festival of youth you are able to get a good night's sleep. The Minimite curls up near you. You may eat provisions before you go to sleep and add 2 STAMINA points (1 point if you have already eaten). Add 3 STAMINA points for the rest. Then turn to 67.

22

Roll 1 die. This is the price, in Gold Pieces, that the merchant is asking for the pipe. If you will pay this price, purchase the instrument. Turn next to 280.

23

A TROLL guard uses this hut as his sentry post. He patrols the area for ten minutes and then sits in his hut for twenty, throughout the day. With a little luck, you will pass by him during one of his twenty-minute rests. If you rolled a:

1 or 2	Turn to 245
3 or 4	Turn to 69
5 or 6	Turn to 99

If you *Tested your Luck* and were Lucky, turn to 167. If you were Unlucky, refer to your single die roll and proceed as instructed above.

24

The crashing shaft behind you makes you run faster along the black passage. Suddenly you gasp as your foot fails to touch the ground below and you fall downwards into a pit! You may cast a spell:

SUD	FAL	RIS	ZEN	SUS
290	399	439	330	424

If you know none of these spells, or prefer not to cast one, turn to 277.

25

You plead with your goddess – but nothing happens! You try again, but she appears not to be listening. A short time later, your captors bundle you out of your cage and towards the large pot, warming over the fire. Three of them pick you up and heave you into the water, which is now uncomfortably warm. Then it happens . . .

Dark clouds rumble in low over the camp. When they are directly overhead they release a torrential downpour which douses the fire and cools your bath. Your bindings slide loose and you are able to scramble from the pot. Libra has not ignored you! The Head Hunters, sensing something supernatural, have scattered into the woods and you are now free to escape. But you may not call on Libra again in this part of your adventure to help you. Not until you reach the city of Kharé will she listen to you.

You collect your belongings and run off into the woods. Turn to 254.

26

You turn down the passage and follow it cautiously for several minutes. You stop to listen and, in the distance, you can hear a low rumbling. You wait to see what happens. The rumbling gets louder and your hair stands on end as you see a large, rounded boulder rolling swiftly down the passage towards you! This rock is almost a perfect fit in the tunnel and its speed is increasing as you dither. Will you use your magic to help you:

GUM	BAM	WAL	FIX	SIT
367	446	323	343	391

Or will you try some other means of escape (turn to 83)? You may call on Libra's help if you have not yet summoned her (turn to 53).

27

By the bridge is a small wooden hut. As you approach, an ugly hunch-backed creature emerges and stands between you and the bridge, barring your way. In a gruff voice he speaks to you:

> 'Halt stranger. If you wish to pass
> Two answers must you give Vancass.'

The guardian of the bridge has dark, glaring eyes but looks no match for you physically, although you suspect he may have magical powers. Do you wish to try answering his questions (turn to 41) or will you instead retrace your steps and take the other path down into the valley (turn to 38)?

28

You walk into the village. Young Hill Dwellers pass you and stare at your strange clothes. Their own attire is rough by comparison and everyone wears their hair long, but piled up on their heads. You pass without incident into the centre of the village. Will you look for an inn for the night (turn to 211) or find an ale-house and relax (turn to 266)?

29

If you offer him an artefact which you have found on your travels, he will accept it, offer you a mug of ale and chat to you (turn to 191). If you cannot offer him an artefact, you must leave immediately and head either for the inn (turn to 92) or out of the village (turn to 21).

30

You rise early to leave Dhumpus. Turn to **208**.

31

Did you eat at all on the first day of your journey since you left Analand? If not, you are feeling very hungry and must lose 3 STAMINA points. Now turn to **246**.

32

You press on through the grass and, after half an hour or so, you reach the river-bank, well upstream of the village you were avoiding. You notice that your backpack feels lighter than normal and you take it off to examine it. Looking inside, you find that you have lost two items of equipment! You must cross off your *Adventure Sheet* any two artefacts that you have collected on your journey (but gold and/or Provisions only if you have nothing else to lose).

As you search for the missing items, the tops of the grasses bend towards you and wrap themselves around your bag, belt and boots. You realize you have been walking through PILFER GRASS which is able to pickpocket items from passing travellers. These two items are now lost for ever. Turn to **231**.

33

You explain that you are travelling to Kharé and ask him for advice on the way ahead. 'I myself have never left this village,' says the man, 'but you have two paths ahead. My advice, though, is not free. For 2 Gold Pieces I will tell you what I know.' If you accept his offer, pay him the money and turn to **225**. If you refuse and wish to press onwards, turn to **81**.

34

You pass along the main path through the village and stop outside a hut where several Hill Dwellers are sitting and eating. They are deep in discussion about something. Will you introduce yourself (turn to **86**) or ignore them and continue (turn to **106**)?

35

You stop at the edge of the village and prepare to bed down for the night. You may eat provisions if you have any. If you do so you may add 2 STAMINA points if this is your first meal of the day (1 point if you have already eaten). You soon drift off but are awakened rudely by three Svinns who hold you to the ground, pinning your arms. They carry you to a small hut at the edge of the village. Turn to **71**.

36

Did you eat at all yesterday? If not, you must lose 3 STAMINA points as you are now very hungry. Continue by turning to **147**.

37

'I'm sure you would, I'm sure you would!' chuckles the little creature. 'But I will come anyway.' You try to swat it away but it is much too quick for you. Faced with no alternative, you continue down the hill with Jann who has hitched a ride on your shoulder. Turn to **111**.

38

The path drops sharply downhill into the valley and then up the other side. The going is very tiring and you must lose 2 STAMINA points. Half-way up the hill is a clearing in which a small wooden hut stands. Throw one die and turn to **23** after you have done so. You may, if you wish, *Test your Luck* although you must do this before turning to **23**.

39

The room is quite large and is evidently a storeroom of some kind. In one corner is a pile of black rocks, and more rocks are held in a bucket near by, these ones glistening dully in the flickering candlelight. In the centre of the room is a strange-shaped mechanical apparatus – perhaps a press or stone-cutter of some kind – and this is being operated by a large, powerful OGRE. He is dropping stones in at one end and turning a metal handle, which crunches the rock. As you enter, the Ogre stops and turns towards you, growling fiercely. Will you run from the room and out of the cave (turn to **144**) or will you face the creature (turn to **285**)?

40

You follow the path carefully downwards, trying to avoid breaking branches as you go. If you wish to stop along the way to eat Provisions, turn to **180**. If you would rather press on, turn to **133**.

41

The hunchback chuckles and asks his first question:

> *'A witch held in captivity*
> *Lives in the woods. First tell to me*
> *If you know of this cunning dame*
> *How is she known; what is her name?'*

What will your answer be:

Allina?	Turn to **238**
Allanna?	Turn to **253**
Alianna	Turn to **143**

If you do not know her name, you may *Test your Luck*. If you are Lucky, you may guess one of the names above. If you are Unlucky or if you would prefer not to *Test your Luck*, turn to **59**.

42

You walk up to the fire in the centre of the village and call out loudly. There is no response. As you wait for some sign of life you begin to feel dizzy. Too late, you realize that the fumes from the fire are overpowering you! You fight to keep consciousness, but without success, and you slump to the ground. Turn to **279**.

43

The broadsword is a fine weapon and you are amazed at your bargain. You may use the sword to fight and may add 1 point to Attack Strength when in use. Turn to **126**.

44

The key opens the lock and you open the cage door to release her. She springs from the cage. 'Stranger, I am indebted to you,' she thanks you. 'And Alianna will reward you!' Do you want a magical item (turn to **248**) or an aid in combat (turn to **122**)?

45

Did you eat at all yesterday? If you ate at the inn or took Provisions, you suffer no penalty, but if you have not eaten during the day you are now hungry and must lose 3 STAMINA points.

There are two ways on from the village of Kristatanti. Choose your path by turning either to **125** or **226**.

46

You continue along the path for most of the afternoon until you reach a gate which is ajar. Turn to **234**.

47

The Goblin senses your defiance and rises, with a large stone club in his hand. You may fight him:

GOBLIN   SKILL 7   STAMINA 6

Turn to **186** if you win. Alternatively, you may cast a spell:

RAZ	BAM	TEL	ZAP	YAG
328	397	309	438	289

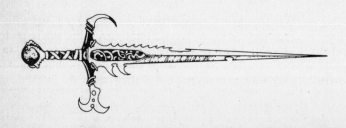

48

You chat to her and drink your – or rather *her* – tea. Suddenly a pain grips your stomach. You wince and cough and are horrified to find you are starting to seize up! Desperately you try to keep moving, but the paralysis drug takes effect. 'Ho, suspicious stranger!' she laughs. 'I can *count* on travellers suspecting my witchcraft!' You are powerless to watch as she goes through your bag looking for magical artefacts. If you have a page from a Spell Book, turn to **77**. Otherwise she will take any two objects in your bag which you know are useful in magic spells and then she magically transports you and your miniature companion (together with the rest of your possessions) out into the woods where the drug eventually wears off (turn to **232**).

49

You may rest if you wish to eat Provisions (if you have any) before your all-night trek. If you take a meal, you may add 2 STAMINA points if you have not already eaten today but only 1 STAMINA point if you have eaten anything. Then you set off. You soon leave the woods following an uphill path and you pause again at daybreak to get your bearings. You must lose 2 STAMINA points for travelling all night without sleep. Turn to **36**.

50

Around the creature's neck is a collar which interests you. It is studded with green gems and looks quite valuable. You may take it if you wish and then you had better leave the village. Turn to **196**.

51

You travel downhill along the valley for an hour, but then the path turns uphill again. The hill you are now climbing is not too steep and as noon approaches you are again on a descending path. You may stop and eat Provisions if you wish and may add 2 STAMINA points if you do. Further along the path in the afternoon, Jann – who has been chattering incessantly to you – warns you to stop. You are being watched. As you are now in a wood, you proceed cautiously. Suddenly the bushes part and a figure steps forward. Dressed in black, this tall man bars your way. Will you prepare to do battle (turn to **117**) or try to talk with him (turn to **103**)?

52

The little creature chatters loudly across the river to its friends. They are obviously not keen that you are refusing their welcome and you decide you had better prepare yourself for defensive action. Turn to **203**.

53

You wait with bated breath. But your prayers are answered as the boulder slows down. It squeals and screeches as invisible brakes take a hold and eventually stop the deadly ball. After a moment, it begins to roll again – but in the opposite direction – and eventually it rolls out of view back up the passage. You decide to return to the main chamber, where you may take either the left-hand (turn to **16**) or the right-hand passage (turn to **3**). Remember you may not call upon Libra again during this adventure.

54

You follow the path for the rest of the afternoon until you stand on a hilltop. The path runs down the hill into a small village set on a river and you follow it down. Turn to **176**.

55

The noise outside eventually subsides as darkness spreads over the village. You have a good night's sleep. Add 3 STAMINA points and turn to **67**.

56

You search through the pockets of the bandits but find nothing there. Setting off again along the path you continue for half an hour until the way ahead becomes an uphill incline. You reach a fork which offers you two ways forward. Turn to **183**.

57

Your brisk walk through the grass ends when your foot kicks a small sack of some kind. Bending down to pick it up, you find it is a pouch containing 12 Gold Pieces! You put this in your backpack. But as you do so, you find you have lost one item that you were carrying. Choose which item you have lost – it may only be gold or Provisions if you had nothing else to lose – and cross it off your *Adventure Sheet*. As you search your pack for this missing object, you notice that the grass is bending towards you and trying to wrap itself round parts of your equipment! You are standing in a meadow of PILFER GRASS and, unless you are careful, it will attempt to steal any items it may pick from your pack. Since you are now aware of this, you may guard your belongings and continue. Turn to **159**.

58

You follow the path for half the morning and reach a fork where you may either continue straight on (turn to **46**) or turn westwards (turn to **10**).

59

The hunchback waves his hand in the air and you feel a sharp pain surge through your body. Lose 2 STAMINA points and 1 LUCK point and return to the junction to take the other path. Turn to **38**.

60

The jewel is large and looks very valuable; it is set in a tarnished mount. His price is 10 Gold Pieces. Buy the jewel if you wish. Turn to **280**.

61

You knock at the door of one of the huts. There is no reply. You may enter anyway (turn to **158**) or try another hut (turn to **271**).

62

You creep off to the edge of the village and settle down under a tree. You may eat Provisions if you wish which will add 2 STAMINA points if this is your first meal of the day or 1 STAMINA point if you have eaten before. You try to sleep under the tree but you are woken continually by strange noises. Add 1 STAMINA point for getting some rest and leave at daybreak. Turn to **45**.

63

You walk down the passage for several minutes. You slip on the dirt and below your feet the ground gives way! You plunge into a hidden pit and land on something soft. Your hand reaches out and touches something which slithers between your fingers. A snake pit! You are sitting on a mound of the deadly reptiles! Will you use your magic to help you:

ZEN	RIS	POP	LAW	FIL
366	417	303	433	344

Or will you look for another means of escape (turn to 165)? If you have not yet used your call to Libra, you had better do so now (turn to 273).

64

No one in the history of the Shamutanti Hills has found a way of escaping the Demon's Deluge and you are not likely to be the first. You are still trying desperately to think of a way out as the air leaves the cave and your lungs fill with water . . .

65

You continue along the path for several hours, taking you deeper into the valley. Presently, the sun begins to set, the air becomes cooler, and you start to consider whether to find a suitable site to camp for the night (turn to 76) or whether to continue onwards without sleep (turn to 224).

66

The door is locked (perhaps as some sort of safety device to seal off the upper parts of the mine from pit disasters – after all, the lives of worker Goblins are expendable), and you will not break through the solid rock. You may either try breaking the door down (turn to 228) or casting a spell:

HUF	HOW	GOP	DOP	DOM
329	423	310	373	350

67

You rise early and leave soon after dawn with Jann still hovering around your head as you set off. Did you eat at all yesterday? If not, you must deduct 3 STAMINA points.

There are two paths ahead: one uphill to the east (turn to **135**), and one downhill to the west (turn to **51**). Which will you choose?

68

You press on, climbing up the hillside for several hours until you are not far from the top. Then you hear a faint sound of bustling activity. Tramping feet, grunting voices and the clanking of metal against rock make you stop and listen. You decide to leave the path and continue cautiously through the woods. A short distance onwards you hide behind a tree and survey a clearing ahead. A number of GOBLINS are in the clearing, in front of an open cave. It appears that they are mining the cave as they trudge in and out of the opening, carrying large bowls full of glistening rocks and dull metallic nuggets. From your position you may easily slip into the cave to see whether you can find anything of value (turn to **175**), or you may ignore the mine and slip around the side to a path leading onwards and down the far side of the hill (turn to **13**).

69

You creep by the sentry post unnoticed. Turn to **237**.

70

Too late, you try to leap clear of the pitfall trap which has opened beneath you. You drop some three metres into the pit and collapse unconscious in a heap. Turn to **139**.

71

You are thrown into the hut and the door is locked. You are their prisoner. You spend half an hour looking for a possible escape but there does not appear to be one. If you wish you may sit down and eat Provisions (add 2 STAMINA points if this is your first meal today; 1 if you have already eaten), then you may either settle down to sleep for the rest of the night (turn to **109**) or keep awake and on your guard in case anything should happen (turn to **140**).

72

Examining the carvings on the axe, you can make out a message which reads: 'This axe was crafted in the Year of the Ox for Glandragor the Protector. Its powers may be realized only by its owner.' It also has the number 233 carved on it. If you keep it as a reserve weapon you must subtract 1 point from your Attack Strength roll when using it. Turn to **126**.

73

The smell gets sweeter as you pass on through the fields of Black Lotus flowers. You feel light-headed as you continue and you start to skip and jump with merriment. Jann, still on your shoulder, is likewise full of glee. Your head swims. Before you can stop yourself, you are feeling dizzy and falling to the ground. You fall into the flowers on to something hard. A surge of horror passes through you as you realize it is a skeleton! But the horror is short-lived as you lose consciousness. The sweet aroma of the Black Lotus is a deadly poison and you have breathed your last. You will rest for ever in the fields of the black death . . .

74

You approach the hut and call through the doorway. No reply. You pull back the drapes and step inside. The hut is obviously an abode of some kind, with pots, pans and clothes strewn about. In front of an open fireplace is a skin rug on the ground and you have not noticed that, as you look around, an eye opens on the skin's head.

Your back is towards the rug and you cannot see it rising up and taking on its natural shape – that of a WOLFHOUND – until it snarls menacingly and attacks. You will have to fight it:

WOLFHOUND   SKILL 7   STAMINA 6

If you win, turn to 50. Or you may fight it with magic:

KIL	YAP	GOB	ZAP	BAG
315	402	425	335	440

75

You leave in search of the local inn. Turn to 134.

76

You find a suitable shelter in the rocks on the bank of the stream and bed down for the night. If you have not eaten since you left the Outpost Settlement, you may take some Provisions if you have any and add 2 STAMINA points. If you have already eaten, you will gain only 1 STAMINA point from the food.

Eventually you drift off to sleep, soothed by the babbling of the stream. A short while later you are awakened by a splashing noise. Looking out from your shelter you see a strange sight. Three small, thin, man-like creatures, glowing with a dull red luminescence, are throwing stones into the stream. Every so often they chirp with glee as a good shot sends a fish flying into the air. As if pulled by a magical force, each fish floats across the water and lands at their feet. Will you sit tight and hope they don't see you (turn to **281**) or stand up and hail them (turn to **12**)?

77

She comes across the Spell Book page and drops your pack. 'My book!' she cries. 'The missing page! Why did you not tell me you had my missing spell?' She scurries off into the kitchen and returns with a cup of liquid which she pours into your mouth. This antidote gradually takes effect, unfreezing your body. She slaps you gently to bring you round. Turn to **114**.

78

'I can give you all sorts of aids for your journey,' she says. 'Are you aligned to the magical or physical arts?' Will you ask her for help with your spells (turn to **17**) or your abilities at swordplay (turn to **240**)?

79

The man shuffles nervously over and shakes your hand. 'Are you magical, stranger?' he asks. 'Are you not afraid of us? Or perhaps you are a healer who can cure us of this *plague*.' At his last word, you spring back, but it is too late. You have made contact with a plague carrier and from now onwards you will lose 3 STAMINA points each day until you either die or you find someone who can cure you of the plague. Deduct your points first thing in the morning. You are horrified at your discovery, back out of the hut and leave the village quickly. Turn to **220**.

80

You enter the village cautiously, creeping round the huts, but the place appears to be deserted. A fire burns in the centre of the camp in a pit and a pile of logs stands near by. Will you look around the huts (turn to **189**) or call out to see whether you can attract someone's attention (turn to **42**)?

81

You pass along the main path through the centre of the village. There is a small inn offering food for sale at which you may stop (turn to **257**) or you may press on through the village (turn to **131**).

82

You creep past the caves. *Test your Luck*. If you are Lucky, turn to **250**. If you are Unlucky, turn to **181**.

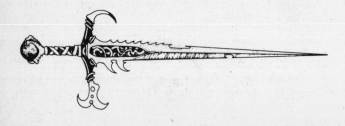

83

Unfortunately for you, there *is* no other way of escape. As you try to think of a plan the boulder is on you, flattening you on the floor. Yet again a Svinn champion has failed to rescue the chief's daughter . . .

84

You must deduct 2 STAMINA points for going without sleep. As you make your way onwards, there is a chance that your noises will attract night creatures. Turn to **123** to see whether you have any encounters, fight if necessary and then *return to this reference*. When you have done this, continue by turning to **31**.

85

You must take 3 STAMINA points' worth of damage as you cover your head and make your way through this downpour of acorns. Turn to **7**.

86

They stop and look at you. They invite you over but become agitated at the sight of your weapon. You may leave your weapon and join them (turn to **185**) or thank them for their offer of hospitality and press on (turn to **106**).

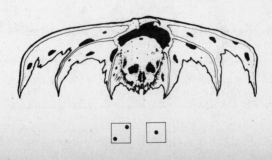

87

In addition, she hands you a bag containing 7 Gold Pieces. Then she chuckles. You turn to leave the house quickly, but she stops you with a hand on your shoulder. 'But Alianna does not give up her prized possessions without a fight!' You turn round to see her casting a spell of some sort over a chair. The chair begins to crack and creak, moving violently in front of you. It forms itself into a WOOD GOLEM which now advances towards you! Will you fight the creature?

WOOD GOLEM   SKILL 8   STAMINA 6

If you win, turn to **169**. Or you may cast a spell:

JIG	DOZ	HOT	KIN	MUG
339	383	297	410	287

88

You stand at the door and call inside. There is no reply. You draw back the drapes and enter the small hut. Cushions ring the room and, as you enter, a strange music played on invisible pipes fills the room. The tune is pleasant and relaxing and you sit down on the cushions. Do you have a musical pipe with you? If so, you may take it out and play along (turn to **11**). Otherwise, turn to **179**.

89

You leap ahead just in time as a pitfall caves in beneath you. You look back to see a gaping pit which you would have fallen into. Turn to **170**.

90

The lock breaks and she jumps from the cage. 'Stranger, I am indebted to you,' she says. 'Alianna will reward you.' Would you like as your reward a magical item (turn to **248**) or an aid in combat (turn to **122**)?

91

You bid the merchant farewell and leave the hut. If you have bought any artefacts from him, you are anxious to know what they are (turn to **126**); but if you bought nothing from him, you may continue on your way (turn to **163**).

92

The inn is not cheap. A bed for the night is 5 Gold Pieces and a meal is 4. If you eat, pay the price and add 2 STAMINA points (1 if you have already eaten today). If you want to sleep here, turn to **55**. If not, you had better leave the village and find a place to bed down (turn to **21**).

93

Roll two dice. If the number rolled is *less than* your SKILL score, you succeed in breaking the door open. If not, then you may try again. Whether or not you succeed, you must deduct 1 STAMINA point at each attempt. If you break the door open, turn to **39**. If you decide to give up your attempts, you may return to the junction and leave the cave (turn to **144**).

94

Surprisingly enough, although you can still feel the force on your arm, it does not hamper your progress and you can make your way onwards. In fact, the going seems to be easier, as if you are being led by some invisible guide who is coaxing you along the best route. Eventually, the going gets easier as the dense undergrowth thins and you are soon walking through a prairie with grass up to your waist. As you leave the heavy foliage, the grip on your arm is released. Add 1 LUCK point. Still you cannot see who, or what, was responsible for the guidance. Turn to **105**.

95

You press onwards, out through Cantopani along the path leading to the Shamutanti Hills. However, you feel a little uneasy while passing the huts on the fringes of the village. Hissings from within and sly faces which disappear from the doorways as you pass make you feel decidedly unwelcome and you are glad to be leaving. At the edge of the town you pass a large boulder and as you do so, two rough-cut villagers spring out with swords drawn. BANDITS! They demand that you hand over your backpack. If you do as they ask, turn to **261**, but if you refuse, you will have to fight them – turn to **104**.

96

You sit down and the young man turns towards you eagerly. Eventually your presence is tolerated at the ale-house and the others get back to drinking and talking. You question the young man about the village. He becomes serious, looks at you grimly and says 'Snattacats!' You ask him what he means, but his reply is silence. Grimly he hangs his head. You try another line of conversation and suddenly he perks up and starts rambling on about his grandmother. The more you talk to him, the more you realize that you have chosen to sit next to the village idiot, hopelessly drunk. After an hour or so you leave the ale-house. Will you look for the inn to spend the night (turn to **211**) or leave the village and sleep rough (turn to **62**)?

97

You may take these Provisions with you. Now turn to **75**.

98

You emerge from the woods on to a river-bank. The path leads over a rough wooden bridge and along the bank. Turn to **231**.

99

As you pass by the sentry post, the Troll emerges from behind the hut, armed with a halberd, and sees you. You will have to fight him:

TROLL   SKILL 8   STAMINA 7

If you win, turn to **177**. If you wish to fight with magic, you may choose:

WOK	SUN	LAM	KIL	DUM
386	363	432	414	317

100

You are lowered down through the blackness until eventually you reach the ground below. If you still have Jann, the Minimite, with you, turn to **286**. Otherwise turn to **197**.

101

You try the key but it does not fit. Turn back to **4** and make another choice.

102

You travel along a path leading upwards a little way until you reach a large natural waterfall. The only path to it leads past a small hut where a ruffian is collecting money. It seems that the price to pay for visiting this waterfall is 3 Gold Pieces. It is a beautiful sight, with large crystal stalactites hanging from the rocks all the way down. Will you pay the price and visit the waterfall (turn to **204**) or return to the village and head for the inn (turn to **92**) or onwards out of town (turn to **21**)?

103

The stranger ignores your words and grips a sharp scimitar. Turn to **117**.

104

The bandits growl and advance. You may fight them in turn:

First BANDIT	SKILL 7	STAMINA 6
Second BANDIT	SKILL 7	STAMINA 8

If you win, turn to **56**.

Alternatively, you may choose a spell:

FOF	JIG	BAM	LAW	YAZ
288	308	327	348	371

If you know none of these spells, draw your weapon and fight the bandits as above.

105

The going is easy through the grass. You happen across a parting where it seems someone has been before, making a trail which is heading in the general direction you wish to continue. Will you follow this path (turn to **57**) or do you mistrust it and wish to make your own way through the grass (turn to **32**)?

106

Further along the way you come across a couple of merchants' huts and you browse through the items for sale. If you wish, and if you can afford it, you may buy any of the following items:

A finely crafted sword	6 Gold Pieces	Turn to **194**
A woven skullcap	4 Gold Pieces	Turn to **247**
Provisions for three meals	6 Gold Pieces	Turn to **97**

If you have no money, you may ask them whether they know of any work that may be going (turn to **229**), or if you don't wish to deal with them at all, you may head for the inn for the night (turn to **134**).

107

For this potion, he demands 4 Gold Pieces and the price is not negotiable. If you wish to buy, pay him the money and take the flask. Otherwise you may refuse his offer. Turn to **280**.

108

You find a suitable spot in the woods to make your camp. If you have not eaten yet today, you may do so if you have Provisions and you will gain 2 STAMINA points. If you have already eaten today you will gain only 1 STAMINA point if you have a meal.

You settle down and sleep, but there is a chance that you may be discovered by night creatures who will disturb your rest. *Remember this reference* (you will have to return here afterwards) and turn to **123** to see whether you encounter anything. You may add 2 points to the die roll you will have to make as night creatures are less likely to approach a camp.

You may set off again the next morning. If you have had a peaceful night's sleep, add 2 STAMINA points. If you encountered any night creatures, you may add only 1 STAMINA point. You follow a path onwards which climbs steadily up a hill. Turn to **36**.

109

You may add 2 STAMINA points for your rest, but if you did not eat at all yesterday you must deduct 3 STAMINA points. You wake early the next morning. Turn to **222**.

110

You pick yourself up off the floor and look around. A shaft of light penetrates the pit and you are relieved to see a passage leading to the daylight outside. Your hand is resting on a furry object which at first you thought was some kind of creature, but now you are able to see that it is a dusty boot. Not far from it is another, and you collect the pair and dust them clean. You now own a pair of fur-skinned boots, which you may take with you. The fur is Borrinskin, and you put the boots in your backpack. Following the passage, you emerge from the mine into the woods by a pathway that runs downhill. Turn to **202**.

111

There seems to be a good deal of merriment in the village. 'It is the festival of the young,' whispers Jann. 'Once a year the children are allowed the freedom of the village. It is a time of great fun and pranks.' A number of children sit in the street ahead, drinking ale. A little too much, it seems, as they are laughing loudly. Ahead a young boy holds an old woman over his knee and is spanking her. A group of boys is fighting outside a hut with a sign which reads: 'Glandragor's Tavern'. A group of girls is standing at a signpost pointing to the 'Crystal Waterfall', tripping up their elders as they pass and giggling to each other. Would you like to avoid this festival and make for the inn (turn to **92**), visit the tavern (turn to **230**), head for the Crystal Waterfall (turn to **102**) or leave town straight away (turn to **21**)?

112

The little men carry you off and you soon arrive at the Head Hunter camp. There is much commotion as you are led into the centre of the settlement. Several natives rush off to fill a large pot with water to be heated over a fire – the implications of which you do not relish! Meanwhile, you are put into a bamboo cage, guarded by a strong warrior. Do you wish to pray to Libra for assistance? If so, turn to **25**. If not, turn to **242**.

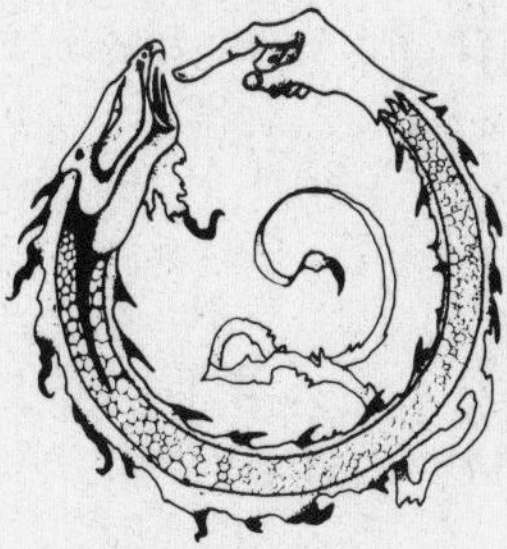

113

The creature jumps in the air as you greet him and cautiously comes closer. Seeing that you mean no harm, he invites you to join with his companions. Will you join them (turn to **216**) or say that you would rather stay where you are and rest (turn to **52**)?

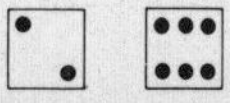

114

'Four days ago I was visited by a traveller such as yourself,' she explains. 'The rogue was leafing through my book when I caught him and as I challenged him he raced off, taking this page with him. He must have been a wizard of some power, considering the speed with which he vanished. I cast an Ageing Spell at him, but it seemed to do no good.' She thanks you for bringing it back and offers to show you how useful it is. She will rid you of the Minimite pest if you wish. If you want to get rid of Jann and regain your ability to use spells, add together the page number you have with the number on what must be the next page and turn to that reference number. If you have not recorded the page number, or if you wish to keep Jann, she allows you to leave and set off again along the path (turn to **232**).

115

You pay the 3 Gold Pieces and settle down for the night. You may add 2 STAMINA points for a refreshing night's sleep. Turn to **30**.

116

The meal is warm and nourishing. Add 2 STAMINA points. Don't forget to pay the price of the meal (1 Gold Piece); continue your journey. Turn to **131**.

117

You prepare to fight the tall ASSASSIN:

ASSASSIN   SKILL 8   STAMINA 6

Or you may cast a spell:

MUG	WOK	ZAP	KIL	FIX
368	452	305	393	342

If you fight and win, turn to **153**. Alternatively you may elect to spare his life when he is reduced to 3 STAMINA points or less, so long as you are clearly winning (i.e. your own STAMINA is at least 6), by turning to **187**.

118

You manage to creep around the creature and, although it snarls menacingly, it does not attack you. Turn to **193**.

119

You open the door. The hut is neatly laid out inside; obviously the touch of a fastidious woman. Chairs are around a table. A mattress lies in one corner and a large kitchen area indicates that whoever lives here is fond of cooking. You hear a cry from a corner hidden by a large cupboard, and as you move over to look you can see a large cage in which a young woman – and quite a pretty one at that – is imprisoned. 'Good stranger,' she pleads, 'let me out of this cage! I have been locked in here for two days by those mischievous Elvins. Can you please help me?' Will you help her (turn to **4**), ask what's in it for you (turn to **78**) or look around the hut for goods to steal (turn to **213**)?

120

You return to the junction and can continue either by taking the other passage (turn to **149**) or by returning to the cave entrance (turn to **144**).

121

Seeing the death of their comrade, the other two Elvins chatter to each other, then rise into the air and nip off. Soon they have disappeared completely. After half an hour they have still not returned, so you gather your possessions together and decide to continue your journey. Turn to **224**.

122

She hands you Ragnar's Armband of Swordmastery. While wearing this item you may add 2 points to your dice roll for Attack Strength if you are using a sword as a weapon. Your powers will be normal if you are using any other weapon. Now turn to **87**.

123

Roll one die to see whether you encounter any night creatures:

Roll	Creature	SKILL	STAMINA
1	Giant Bat	5	5
2	Giant Bat	5	5
3	Wolfhound	7	6
4	Werewolf	8	9
5+	No encounter		

You must fight any creatures you encounter. The following spells may be used:

RAN	GUM	LAW	WIK	BIG
396	421	448	437	453

After checking your encounter, return to the previous reference.

124

'You cannot escape the Spirit of Mananka!' cries the face. 'And your mission is cursed!' You watch as the smoke contracts and disappears back inside the box. You wonder at the Spirit's curse, but there is little you can do. Until you find some way of ridding yourself of this curse, your STAMINA has been weakened. Each time you lose STAMINA points for any reason *except casting spells*, you must lose 1 *extra* STAMINA point. You may search for some means of ridding yourself of the Spirit's curse for, until you do, you are more vulnerable to dangers. You may now leave the hut and continue your journey onwards. Turn to **196**.

125

You leave Kristatanti along a path which snakes out into the hills. All morning you follow it as it twists through the woods of gnarled trees until eventually you reach a clearing where another path joins from the east. A signpost at the junction indicates straight on to Dhumpus and westwards to Alianna. Will you continue onwards (turn to **54**) or westwards (turn to **154**)?

126

You may investigate your purchases by turning to the appropriate references as indicated: the potion (**274**); the broadsword (**43**); the pipe (**249**); the axe (**72**); the bag of teeth (**190**); and the jewel (**152**).

You will return here after investigating all your new acquisitions. To continue onwards, turn to **95**.

127

You follow a meandering path around the side of a hill for most of the morning. You may stop and eat Provisions along the way if you wish and you will gain 2 STAMINA points if you do. As noon approaches you can see the path offering you two ways onwards. One path follows the hill downwards into a shallow valley and then climbs the next hill. Your other choice is a path which leads to a rope-and-wood bridge which spans the hills. Will you cross this bridge (turn to **27**) or follow a course down the hillside (turn to **38**)?

128

You dash on ahead but suddenly realize you are running into an unknown mine with perhaps your only exit sealed off behind you! If you wish to continue downwards, turn to **24**. Otherwise you may turn round and head back for the door (turn to **66**).

129

The driver is a cheerful fellow and prefers company to travelling alone. You may add 1 LUCK point for getting this lift. You travel for most of the morning at a pace not much faster than you could walk until he finally reaches a field where he is collecting vegetables. You may offer to help him for an hour or so in return for the lift (turn to **173**) or you may leave him and continue your journey (turn to **46**).

130

The door opens slowly until, at one point, a catch clicks and some ominous rumblings start. Behind you, a wall is rising through the floor to seal off your escape. A great splashing makes you whirl round and you gasp as you see hundreds of gallons of water come gushing around you from within the room! You are swept off the ground as the room and corridor fill. If you do not react quickly you will be drowned as the water fills all the available space. Will you cast a spell:

SUS	HUF	DIP	FOF	SUD
390	324	416	365	445

Or do you have another plan (turn to **64**)? If you have not yet called on help from your goddess, you may do so now (turn to **260**).

131

You continue along the path, leaving the village behind. About half an hour later, you reach the start of the climb into the hills and continue upwards. Five minutes later, you reach a fork offering you two ways onwards. Turn to **183**.

132

They release your hands, allowing you to choose a spell to impress them with:

KID	JAP	DUD	GOB	SIX
353	376	292	401	316

If you know none of these, turn to **218**.

133

You continue along the trail and the undergrowth around you gets thicker. Suddenly there is a cracking beneath your feet and something gives way underfoot. You may *Test your Luck*. If you are Unlucky, turn to **70**. If you are Lucky, turn to **89**. If you would prefer not to *Test your Luck*, turn to **70**.

134

The inn charges 3 Gold Pieces for a hearty meal and 3 Gold Pieces for a bed. If you can afford it, you may eat. The meal (Hillfox broth and rice) will restore 3 STAMINA points if you have not yet eaten today or 2 STAMINA points if this is not your first meal. If you wish to stay at the inn for the night, turn to **115**. If you cannot afford it or will not pay, you may leave the village in search of a suitable place to camp for the night (turn to **14**).

135

You travel along the path for some time. Passing out of a shrubby woodland a pleasant smell hits your nostrils. Off to the right is a field of beautiful black flowers. The path through the field leads on over the brow of the hill into a valley below. Jann believes this is the quickest path to Torrepani, the next village on your route. If you don't trust his judgement you may use a spell:

FIF	SUD	HUF	MAG	SUS
435	341	419	321	394

Or you may continue onwards (turn to **73**). Alternatively, you may retrace your steps and take the other route downhill from Birritanti (turn to **51**).

136

If this is your first meal today, add 2 STAMINA points. If you have already eaten, add only 1 STAMINA point. You rest for half an hour or so and then continue your journey. Turn to **65**.

137

You continue through the bush until you reach a point where the undergrowth thins and becomes a waist-high grassland. Turn to **105**.

138

The passage continues until you reach a large stone-cut door blocking your progress. Will you try the door handle (turn to **255**) or return to the junction and take the other passage (turn to **149**)?

139

When you regain consciousness, you are bound hand and foot. The excited jabberings of a small group of black-skinned HEAD HUNT-ERS around you make you fear for your life. You may try to cast a spell:

RIS	DUD	HOT	KID	WIK
357	406	333	450	379

Or you may wait to see what they intend to do with you (turn to **112**).

140

You remain diligently awake, watching the door, but no one comes during the night. Lose 2 STAMINA points for not sleeping and a further 3 STAMINA points if you did not eat yesterday. Turn to **222**.

141

The strange carvings are in a familiar language, but the quality of the shaft and head indicate that the axe is well used and may not last many more battles. The merchant wants 7 Gold Pieces for the weapon. You may pay his price and take the axe, or you may bargain. If you wish to bargain, roll two dice. A roll lower than 7 indicates you are a hard bargainer and he will accept this roll, in Gold Pieces, as his price. If you roll over 7, your bartering angers him and he insists on raising the price to this level. Buy if you will, then turn to **280**.

142

You draw your weapon and try to smash the lock. Roll two dice and compare the total with your SKILL score. If the roll is lower than your SKILL, you succeed in breaking the lock and releasing the woman (turn to **90**). If the roll equals or exceeds your SKILL, the lock remains intact. Each time you try, the blow blunts your weapon and you must deduct 1 point from your SKILL when you use this weapon. If you have two weapons, you may use the less favoured one so as to suffer no penalty when using your normal weapon. You must try at least once but, after this, you may stop at any time, give up and leave the house (turn to **278**).

143

The hunchback smiles.

> *'Your answer is correct and true.*
> *Now you must answer question two:*
> *Through villages three you now have passed*
> *What was the first, second and last?'*

How will you answer him?

Cantopani, Kristatanti and Dhumpus	Turn to **262**
Kristatanti, Birritanti and Dhumpus	Turn to **253**
Cantopani, Gorretanti and Dhumpus	Turn to **59**

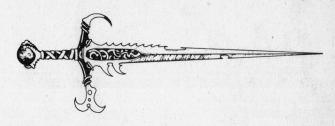

144

You emerge carefully from the cave, trying not to be spotted by wandering Goblins. *Test your Luck.* If you are Lucky, turn to **259**. If you are Unlucky, turn to **217**.

145

Both boxes look like fairly uninteresting wooden cases, each fastened with a catch. Will you try opening the one on the left (turn to **251**) or the right (turn to **258**)?

146

The tea is refreshing and you may add 1 STAMINA point. Also add 1 LUCK point for making the right choice. You notice that the woman is cursing and her actions are becoming slower. She creeps slowly off into the kitchen and you see her gulping down another drink. Then she comes back and questions you about your journey. She is particularly interested in knowing whether you came across an old man. If you have with you a page from a Spell Book, turn to **184**. If not, turn to **219**.

147

The gentle upward slope becomes a steep climb and you must rest several times during the morning. Finally you reach the top and can look over the hill to see that the path leads into a small settlement of crudely made huts. You follow the path down and into the village. As you arrive, the villagers notice you and make for their huts, almost as if in fear. They are a sorry-looking bunch, short and squat with tough, leathery skin. Several of them are missing limbs and some are only able to drag themselves along with their hands. Will you try to talk with the villagers (turn to **61**) or continue onwards through the village (turn to **220**)?

148

Have you eaten since leaving the Outpost Settlement yesterday? If not, you are extremely hungry and must deduct 3 STAMINA points for going without food for the day.

You continue on your way and approach a rope bridge strung precariously between two boulders. You may either continue along the path on your side of the water (turn to **209**) or you may cross the river on the bridge and follow a path running over a small hill (turn to **19**).

149

The passage twists round to the right until it finally ends at a doorway. Will you try the door (turn to **268**) or leave the cave entirely (turn to **144**)?

150

You press on through the wood and soon come across another path which crosses it. You follow this path northwards until you come to a junction. A signpost at the junction points westwards to Alianna and straight on to Dhumpus. Will you head for Alianna (turn to **154**) or Dhumpus (turn to **54**)?

151

Some way down the corridor you hear whimpering and your torch lights up a frail shape. Hiding in the shadows is the young Svinn girl! You take her up and comfort her, and she clings to you for safety. Now all you have to do is escape! Turn to **195**.

152

The glittering jewel in its mount is cold to the touch but has an unusual sparkle. You put it in your pack. However, it is in fact an Ice Jewel and sometime later will melt away to worthless liquid. You have wasted your money. Turn to **126**.

153

Looking through his pockets you find 3 Gold Pieces. You may now set off ahead, continuing along the path. Turn to **212**.

154

Some way down the path you come across a hut in a rather pictur-esque setting, among trees with leaves of contrasting shades of green. Flowers decorate the walls of the hut and the door is painted in ornate designs. You approach the door and knock but there is no reply. Will you enter the house (turn to **119**) or leave well alone (turn to **278**)?

155

Searching the bodies, you find a miserable 2 Gold Pieces in their pockets. You may also take 8 teeth, which lie on the ground next to the first Goblin. Turn to **202**.

156

You climb into the undergrowth from the path and plan a wide sweep around the village. The going is heavy as you climb through the vegetation. Bushes and tall grasses are constant obstacles which catch and scratch you. Suddenly you feel a strong hand on your arm which makes you whirl round – but you can see nothing gripping you! Will you try to continue (turn to **94**) or prepare to defend yourself (turn to **241**)?

157

The path winds upwards into the hills and you enter a wood. The afternoon sun glints through the trees, playing tricks on your eyes. Every so often you catch a glimpse of some strange-shaped animal or other watching you, only to find that it is the silhouetted branches and leaves caught at an odd angle. You reach a position where you may rest and eat Provisions if you wish (turn to **18**). If you wish to continue, turn to **210**.

158

Inside, the hut has no furniture. A small fire burns in the middle of the floor and against the far wall stands a family of three, cowering away from you. Will you hold out your hand in friendship (turn to **79**) or cast a spell:

GAK	FOF	RAN	FAM	DOC
385	431	337	413	299

Alternatively you may leave the village (turn to **220**).

159

Further along the path, you come across another object, this time a locket containing a small portrait of a woman, obviously pilfered from a previous traveller unaware of the grass's habits. You may take this with you. Eventually you reach the river-bank again, well past the village. Turn to **231**.

160

You pray to your goddess and, amidst the crashing of rubble, you can hear a great creaking as the door slowly opens. When it has opened wide enough, you nip through it into the room, just in time, as you hear a great crashing from the tunnel. Return to the junction – turn to **120**.

You have now called on Libra for help, your one and only time allowable in the Shamutanti Hills. Should you attempt to seek her assistance again between here and Kharé, she will ignore you (i.e. you may not choose this option if it is given in the text). You are on your own!

161

The meal is just being served. If you wish to sit down to eat, pay the 2 Gold Pieces and have your bowl of Skunkbear stew. You may add 3 STAMINA points if you eat. You will not be able to eat your own Provisions at the inn. If you wish to rest for the night, pay the 3 Gold Pieces. The bed you are given is not particularly clean, but is comfortable and you may add 5 STAMINA points for a good night's rest.

If you wished to eat, but not rest, turn to **62**. If you have stayed the night, turn now to **45**.

162

You must fight the Giant:

HILL GIANT   SKILL 9   STAMINA 11

If you win, turn to **265**. Alternatively you may cast a spell:

YOB	KIL	DUM	BIG	YAZ
361	430	338	411	384

163

The villagers are becoming curious about you and you decide to make your way onwards. Following the path out of Cantopani you approach the Shamutanti Hills themselves. After half an hour or so, a fork in the path gives you a choice of two ways. Turn to **183**.

164

The path winds alongside a bubbling stream and you follow it onwards along the west bank. The valley you are in becomes narrower, but you soon come across a flat, grassy bank where you may stop and eat Provisions (turn to **136**). If you would prefer to continue, turn to **65**.

165

You may try to kill all the snakes in the pit with your weapon. *Test your Luck*. If you are Lucky, *Test your Luck* again. You must keep trying until you are Lucky three times in succession. Each time you are Unlucky you are bitten by a snake for 3 STAMINA points of damage. If you are Lucky three times in succession, you manage to kill all the snakes and may turn to **206**.

166

Which spell will you choose?

NAP	SIX	BAG	LAW	KIL
332	295	313	380	427

If you do not know these spells, or prefer not to use one, you will have to use your weapon. Turn to **20**.

167

Turn to **245**.

168

You turn to your pack and pick it up. But you drop it again in fear as it moves in your hands! Something is inside it! Cautiously, you open the top and, as you do so, a green squirrel-like creature with a huge belly leaps out and into the woods. You curse and examine the contents, but it is too late: the little creature has eaten all your Provisions. You are angry at your own carelessness and set off briskly along the trail again. Turn to **210**.

169

Hurriedly, you leave the house and follow the path back to the junction where you may head north towards Dhumpus. Turn to **54**.

170

Your relief is somewhat premature, however, as you discover when you take your next step forward. Your foot triggers a release mechanism and three saplings snap up in front of you. Each is fitted with sharpened stakes which whip towards you at heart level. You are impaled on this fiendish device and your journey has ended here. Your head will soon join the others on the posts you have just passed . . .

171

The creature is a MINIMITE and calls itself Jann. It is very friendly and tells you you are looking down on Birritanti, the largest village in the Shamutanti Hills. Birritanti is a friendly village, where all travellers spend at least one night. Consequently, prices are a little on the high side. The Minimite would like to come with you. Will you allow it to stay on your shoulder and follow the path down into Birritanti (turn to **111**) or will you tell it you would rather travel alone (turn to **37**)?

172

You call into the hut but there is no reply. Parting the drapes, you look in. A low table and three stools are in the middle of the floor and two boxes stand on the table. Will you enter and investigate the boxes (turn to **145**) or try one of the other two huts, the green one (turn to **88**) or the brown (turn to **74**)?

173

He is grateful for the help and offers you vegetables to take with you on your journey – enough for one meal – as payment. Then you leave him and set off along the path. Turn to **46**.

174

Further along the corridor you come to a door. Will you try the door (turn to **130**) or return to the junction and take the other passage (turn to **151**)?

175

You creep closer, round the side of the hill, to the entrance of the cave. You seize your chance when all is quiet to nip inside and hide in the shadows. Following the passage cautiously, you come to a junction where you may fork to the left (turn to **138**) or the right (turn to **149**). Which will you choose?

176

As you follow the path downwards you pass a sign. You are entering the village of Dhumpus. Will you find an inn to rest for the night (turn to **134**) or try to make contact with the villagers (turn to **34**)?

177

You search the Troll's body and hut. Inside the hut you find a pouch containing 3 Gold Pieces. Around the Troll's neck is a small amulet made of twisted metal. This is a Lucky Charm – although it brought little luck to the Troll. While wearing this charm, you may subtract one point from your dice roll each time you *Test your Luck*. Turn to **237**.

178

The path winds through fields of wild scrubland. The countryside is deserted and an eerie silence is broken only by the cawing of an occasional crow. The birds appear to pause in the air to examine you as they pass and you feel uneasy in their presence. You pass over a small hillock, from the top of which you can see the path continuing downwards into a small settlement of huts at the base of the Shamu-tanti Hills. You follow the path and, as you approach the village, noises and movements indicate that it is populated. As the path runs straight through the village, you have little choice but to follow it.

The round huts are made of a hard-baked, bright clay with thatched roofs. As you pass, eyes appear at dark doorways watching your movements. Suddenly a villager appears from one of the dwellings and stands before you. He is five feet tall with thick-set arms and thighs half clothed in tattered breeches. His eyes are wild and his long red hair and beard stand out on his face in a wiry tangle. 'Halt, stranger!' he commands. 'What business have you in Cantopani?' What is your response?

Tell him you are a trader	Turn to **264**
Ask for directions onwards	Turn to **33**
Tell him you are hungry and need Provisions	Turn to **198**

179

You realize that a few more minutes of this music and you will be dropping off to sleep. But the effect is so relaxing that you cannot help yourself. Slowly you drift away. Turn to **279**.

180

You pick a clearing where you may open your backpack and get out your Provisions. Your ears are peeled to the sounds around you and you are startled when a flock of Woodgulls fly up into the air near by. You may, if you wish, pack up your bags and continue your trek (turn to **133**) or stay to finish your meal (turn to **272**).

181

You step on a twig which snaps loudly. A stirring comes from within one of the caves and a noise indicates something is approaching. A large figure emerges in ragged clothes and you now face a GIANT, armed with a heavy club. Will you prepare to attack the creature (turn to **162**) or attempt to talk with it (turn to **256**)?

182

What will you give the man? If you have an axe, turn to the number carved on the axe. If you do not have an axe, you will now have to give him something else (turn to **29**).

183

You ponder the two trails. As you consider the paths onwards, you hear weak cries from a large tree ahead of you. Cautiously, you step up to see an old man sitting on the lowest branch, apparently afraid to jump down to the ground, which considering his age is not surprising. He pleads with you to assist and you help him down. It transpires that he has been travelling from Dhumpus and is headed towards the Outpost Settlement in Analand. His journey had been safe enough until he was waylaid by Elvins, robbed, and left in the tree. In return for your kindness, he relates a rhyme which he feels may help you:

> 'See him though he sees you not;
> The black-eyed creature creeps.
> A guardian once, but now his lot:
> The key to freedom keeps.'

He is not sure exactly what the rhyme signifies, but he knows that the Elvins are particularly keen on finding the key in question. He also presses on you his only possession: a page from a Spell Book (page number 102). The spell described is incomplete; you have only part of it. Looking at it, it appears to be some sort of pest-repelling spell. He then bids you farewell and heads off towards Cantopani.

You may now choose your way onwards. Will you take the high way up into the hills (turn to **157**) or the low way along the valley (turn to **164**)? Alternatively you may investigate a buzzing coming from around the tree (turn to **200**).

184

You describe the old man you encountered and her eyes light up. She asks whether you stole from him a page from a Spell Book and is overjoyed as you pull the page from your pack. Giggling with glee, she snatches it from you. Turn to **114**.

185

You sit and talk with them. They seem to be amongst the senior members of the village society and this has been a lucky encounter (add 2 LUCK points). They offer you food, which you may eat for a gain of 1 STAMINA point. As the conversation becomes lighter, you jokingly refer to the 'buffoons at Kristatanti', a comment which does not go down well with one of your hosts who happens to be from that village. In anger, he rises and challenges you. As you are on his own territory this would not be a wise challenge to accept, so you back off. He chases you angrily through Dhumpus and you flee before him. On the edge of the village he gives up the chase and you may head onwards – but you realize with dismay that you have left your weapon behind! You must now continue weaponless and, unless you have a reserve in your pack, you must deduct 4 SKILL points until you find another weapon. Turn to 14.

186

There is little in the room of value, but the dead Goblin wears a silver key around its neck with the number 111 on it. You may take this key with you and continue either onwards through the door ahead (turn to 239) or back the way you came (turn to 120).

187

He begs for mercy and, when you step back from the battle, he is overwhelmingly grateful. Picking himself up and nursing his wounds he tells you he is Flanker, an assassin and thief. He always picks on wayfarers for combat practice and thought you would be no match. He too is headed for Kharé and, in return for your mercy, he promises he will remain your friend. This will be a valuable asset in the cityport. When you reach Kharé you will meet Flanker again and he promises he will aid you. Turn to reference 79 in the second *Sorcery!* adventure to find out how he will help. He will not accompany you to Kharé and instead disappears into the woods. You have made a valuable contact here. Add 2 LUCK points and continue by turning to 212.

188

Soon it becomes dark and you must decide whether to set up camp for the night (turn to 108) or to continue without rest (turn to 49).

189

All the huts have brightly coloured drapes hanging in their doorways, and each is a different colour. You may investigate one with a red doorway (turn to 172), a green doorway (turn to 88) or a brown doorway (turn to 74).

190

The teeth in the bag are indeed from various creatures: several from Death-hounds, three from an Ape, four from a Goblin, two from a

Snattacat and a large molar from a Giant. You may take any or all of these, then turn to **126**.

191

You chat for some time. When you tell him you are heading for Kharé he tells you that you will have to pass through Torrepani and that you will find it a different place as the Svinns that live there seem to be in a permanent state of depression these days. Through Torrepani you have a day's travel to Kharé and the going is easy down the hills. You can add 2 STAMINA points for the ale and 1 LUCK point for the information. Jann, the Minimite, has been sipping at your ale and is now quite drunk. You try to creep off either to the inn (turn to **92**) or out of the village (turn to **21**) but you cannot lose the little creature.

192

You sit down and mutter some comment about the mud on the trails at this time of year. The old man grunts in agreement. Eventually the silence gives way to noisy chatter once more and you talk to the old man. He is a hill farmer on the outskirts of the village and sees much of what comes and goes in Kristatanti. He has heard of the capture of the Crown of Kings but has little interest in world affairs. You tell him a little of yourself and soon you are both laughing heartily as you exchange Goblin jokes. Eventually, he stands to leave. 'There are two ways onwards from Kristatanti, stranger,' he says. 'One will take you past Alianna's home – and you will need your wits about you if she is there. The other leads up into the hills to the Lea-Ki, domain of the great ones. I wish you the luck of Sindla on your journey. Perhaps this will help you on your way.' He hands you an apple-like fruit which he has grown on his farm. It is a nourishing Bomba and, if you eat this along with a normal meal, it will double your gain in STAMINA. You thank him and wish him a good night.

You may add 2 LUCK points for your encounter. Then you must decide whether to spend the night in the inn (turn to **211**) or wander off into the woods outside the village to sleep rough (turn to **62**).

193

You continue onwards, up the path for a couple of hours, down another valley and back up another hill. It is now late afternoon and you begin to think about where you will stay for the night. Ahead of you, however, is a small village set into the hill. Turn to **28**.

194

The sword has a specially sharpened blade and will inflict 3 STAMINA points' worth of damage instead of the normal 2. However, you will not be able to take this sword if you already have a sword unless you leave your old one behind. If you don't consider this new sword is as good as your old one, you may ask the merchant for your money back (*Test your Luck* – if you are Lucky he will give you a refund). Then turn to **75**.

195

Behind you a roaring puts you on your guard. The walls of the corridor begin to shake and crumble and you are forced to venture further to avoid the collapse which is sealing off your exit. Ahead of you now, a narrow shaft of light gives you cause for hope. Perhaps this is another exit? The roaring sound gets louder as you step from the corridor into a large cavern. Suddenly you gasp as you back against the wall, shielding the child from the sight you have seen.

Standing before you on four legs is a huge MANTICORE – a hybrid creature with a lion's body and a scorpion's tail. Its face is that of an old man and as it sees you it rears back, flapping two great wings. Will you fight the creature (turn to **227**) or cast a spell?

PEP	BAG	HOP	FOF	DOZ
302	389	345	415	325

196

Cautiously, you leave the village and follow the river upstream for an hour. Turn to **231**.

197

You peer around in the blackness. The Svinns throw you down a torch and tinderbox to light your way. Lighting up the torch you can see you are in a large cavern. Two passageways lead onwards. Will you take the one on the right (turn to **3**) or the left (turn to **16**)?

198

He motions on ahead, telling you that you will find the village inn shortly on the right.

By choosing this option, you will now discover one of the rules of the game which you will otherwise only discover by trial and error. The adventure is divided into *days* and each day you will need to eat one meal, otherwise you will lose STAMINA points due to undernourishment. Options will be given either to eat Provisions from your pack or to buy food at local inns during the day. If you go for a day without food, you will suffer. When night comes, you will be given the option to sleep or continue through the night. Likewise, if you miss a night's sleep you will also lose STAMINA points as you will be tired the next day, although taking a night's rest will usually replenish your STAMINA. But you will have to choose your times to eat and sleep carefully as sometimes a seemingly 'safe' place to rest and eat may hold hidden dangers!

You walk on ahead as the villager indicated. Turn to **257**.

199

The key is old and rusty and a number is stamped into it. You can just make out the figure on the key: 54. You may put this in your backpack and then either leave the village quickly (turn to **196**) or try the other box on the table (turn to **251**).

200

As you look up, you can see a beehive around which a small swarm of bees are buzzing. You may climb up the tree to investigate (turn to **270**) or ignore it and continue onwards (turn to **9**).

201

The job is indeed unpleasant. The villager feeds you (add 2 STAMINA points) but you lose 3 STAMINA points for missing a night's sleep. You may, if you wish, use your magic to help you with the job:

BIG	DIP	PEP	FIL	ZAP
298	444	362	412	318

Otherwise turn to **263**.

202

You leave the mine along the path downwards through the woods. Continuing for a couple of hours – it is now late afternoon – you are relieved to see a small village ahead of you, set into the hillside. Turn to **28**.

203

Sensing your attitude, the creature pulls a short sword from its belt. It drops sharply out of the air and nips in at you, slashing at your arm with its weapon. Its speed astounds you and before you realize what has happened, the sharp sword has grazed your arm, inflicting 1 STAMINA point's worth of damage. You may fight this little ELVIN, but during the fight its speed adds two points to its dice roll when calculating Attack Strength:

ELVIN   SKILL 6   STAMINA 4

If you win, turn to **121**. Alternatively you may cast a spell:

HOT	ZEL	WOK	BIG	YAZ
405	294	441	356	378

204

The ruffian takes your 3 Gold Pieces and hands you a piece of cloth to use as a towel. Along with two other villagers – and of course Jann the Minimite – you take off your clothes and bathe in the waterfall. You begin to glow and the cool water is not only refreshing but also invigorating. You are bathing in a waterfall with magical healing properties. You may restore your SKILL, STAMINA and LUCK scores to their *Initial* values for washing away your wounds. The waterfall will also cure you of any diseases you may have picked up (but not curses). Then you must return to the village where you pass the inn. Turn to **92**.

205

Squealing loudly, the Minimite disappears from your shoulder. You are relieved to find that you will be able to make use of your magic once more. The old woman allows you to leave and you continue along the path. Turn to **232**.

206

You are surrounded by dead snakes. Your luck held out, but your success will not. You have no means of climbing back up to the passage! The rest of your life will now be spent starving to death – although if you can stomach raw snake you will live a little longer . . . Your only remaining chance is if you have not yet called upon Libra (turn to **273**).

207

You enter the cave and can hear a faint whistling which gets louder the deeper you go. A little deeper still into the cave you stumble and fall, and as you do so, the whistling stops. To your horror you realize you have tripped over an enormous foot and, in front of you, a GIANT is rubbing its eyes and looking towards you! It grabs a club and picks itself slowly up. You will have to fight it, either with a weapon:

HILL GIANT   SKILL 9   STAMINA 11

(if you win, turn to **265**), or with a spell:

KIL	BIG	YAZ	YOB	DUM
430	411	384	361	338

208

You may leave the village along one of two paths. One winds up into the hills – turn to **147** if you wish to take this one. The other takes a downhill route into a wood – turn to **127** to follow this one.

209

You continue along a riverside path for several hours until you reach a wide bend. In the elbow of the bend ahead you can see a cluster of huts made out of thatched branches and twigs. A fire in the centre of the huts wafts smoke into the air, but not a sound comes from the village. Will you continue ahead into the village (turn to **80**) or leave the path and go up into the hills to try to avoid it (turn to **156**)?

210

The climb continues for two or three hours as the path twists this way and that up the hillside. Soon the air gets cold and the sun sets, making it difficult for you to see. However, the moon is full and will be able to light the way as it gets darker. Would you like to continue further, marching through the night (turn to **84**) or will you stop and make camp to get some sleep (turn to **283**)?

211

The village inn will charge you 3 Gold Pieces for a night's rest and 2 Gold Pieces for nourishing food. If you wish to buy either of these, turn to **161**. If the price is too high for you, turn to **62**.

212

Continuing along the path and round the side of a hill, you are now becoming increasingly irritated by the Minimite's chattering. You come across a small wooden hut where an old woman sits on the front step. As you pass she calls out to you, inviting you over. Will you see what she wants (turn to 243) or ignore her and continue (turn to 235)?

213

She curses as you search the hut. This curse, however, is no idle threat. The Curse of Alianna reduces your SKILL score by 2 points from now until such time as the curse is removed. Quickly you look through drawers and cupboards but succeed only in finding a pouch containing soft brown sand, and 2 Gold Pieces. You may take these with you, leave the house and set off again. Turn to 278.

214

The sword has a fine cutting edge and has been honed by a master craftsman. Roll two dice. This is the price in Gold Pieces that the merchant requires for the sword. If you are prepared to pay this price you may purchase it. Whether or not you do, turn next to 280.

215

Three Svinns chase you as you run down the hill. They tackle and grapple with you, finally pinning you down. Lose 2 STAMINA points for the struggle. They tie you into the rope basket and lower you down the pit. Turn to 100.

216

The creatures are ELVINS, mischievous little half-humans. They live in a village not far up the river and they are fond of impish pranks. Every so often they will disappear and, as you search round nervously, reappear suddenly in front of you just to make you jump. They are able to turn their glow on and off at will, and another favourite trick is to extinguish their glow and drop down in front of you. More often than not, this means you trip over them, causing considerable merriment to all but you. Nevertheless, you keep your temper. You do appear to be hindering their progress and after an hour or so they tire of you and vanish into the woods along the riverside. You wait in vain for them to reappear and eventually decide to find another suitable shelter for the night to get some sleep. You awake again at sunrise and continue along the path. Turn to 148.

217

You have been unlucky and are noticed by a small group of 3 Goblins who come at you armed with picks:

FIRST GOBLIN	SKILL 5	STAMINA 4
SECOND GOBLIN	SKILL 6	STAMINA 4
THIRD GOBLIN	SKILL 5	STAMINA 5

Attack each in turn and, if you win, turn to **155**. Or you may cast a spell:

HOP	ZAP	RAP	RAW	RAZ
428	**407**	**358**	**381**	**442**

218

They have taken your backpack and are sorting through it, taking any items they wish. Having done this, and regarding you as fairly harmless, they let you go.

To decide which items they want, go through all the items you possess one by one and *Test your Luck* on each. Each time that you are Lucky, the item in question is no use to them and you may keep it. Each time you are Unlucky they will steal this item from you and you must cross it off your Equipment List. Include your Gold – and your Provisions – as single items. You do not have to deduct LUCK points each time you *Test your Luck* here.

When they have ransacked your possessions, they let you go and you may leave the village. Turn to **196**.

219

She asks you whether you have any items 'of a magical nature'. You are naturally a little suspicious and avoid the issue. Eventually she allows you to leave and continue your journey. Turn to **232**.

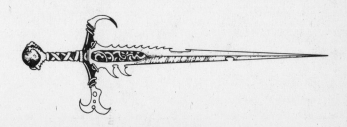

220

Some way down the hill you stop for a rest. You sit on a boulder to survey what lies ahead. The path leads downwards into a vale. Cradled between three hills is a village – and quite a large one at that. The sun is falling rapidly and you decide to head downwards towards this settlement. An overhanging branch touches your face and you hear a lively chirping. Hovering by your shoulder is a small creature the size of your thumb. It is child-like but very thin, with green skin, and it flits around you on transparent wings. It seems to be quite friendly and alights on your shoulder. You may talk to it (turn to 171) or try to get rid of it with a spell:

SIX	WIK	HOP	GAK	WAL
387	336	451	300	306

221

The cave is not deep and appears to be empty. Rubble, mostly small pebbles, on the floor includes some large items such as a huge broken stool, a net with a very wide mesh and a large skull, human-shaped but well over normal size. All of this leads you to one conclusion: these caves are inhabited by Giants! You may take anything – or any part of anything – on the floor that you wish with you, but if you take the stool, you will not be able to carry anything else so you will have to leave all your other possessions except your weapon. Then you may leave and go either into the other cave (turn to 207) or leave the caves and continue onwards (turn to 250).

222

An hour after daybreak you hear noises outside. The door opens and five Svinns come in followed by an old man with grey hair and colourful robes. He announces himself as Proseus, the Svinn chief, and apologizes for having captured you. He nods to a menial who brings in bread and milk. You may eat this meal and add 2 STAMINA points.

The chief explains that you have a mission of the utmost importance ahead of you. His young daughter, his only heir, has been captured by marauders and is being offered as a sacrifice to a powerful cave demon. Several of his own men have tried to rescue the girl but so far with no success. 'We are a desperate people,' explains the chief. 'You must be our champion and rescue our heir. If you succeed you may choose your own reward.'

It is clear that, in spite of the chief's apparent good nature, you have little choice in this matter. You are taken out of the village and along a meandering path up another hill. On the top of the hill is a hole in the ground and the Svinns prepare a basket to lower you down into what must be a secret entrance to the demon's cave. Will you try a last attempt at escaping (turn to **215**) or are you thinking only of the rich treasures you may win (turn to **100**)?

223

As you move, the creature steps towards you, showing its sharp teeth. Realizing you cannot avoid it without a fight, you step forward. Turn to **252**.

224

You must lose 2 STAMINA points for continuing through the night without rest. Just before sunrise you pause briefly to take your bearings in the morning light. Turn to **148**.

225

He places the coins in a pouch around his waist. 'The low way leads through the Vale of the Elvin,' he tells you, 'and unless you are prepared for Elvin ways – for they are mischievous and magical – you had better avoid this path. The high way takes you up into the hills past the Schanker Mines.' He laughs, and adds: 'But you must keep your head if you take this path! Head onwards for Kristatanti, which you will reach in a day or two, for few villages in the Shamutanti Hills welcome strangers, and at Kristatanti you will at least find food and shelter. And beware the Black Lotus on your travels – its sweet aroma is deadly.' You thank him for his advice and press onwards. Turn to **81**.

226

You leave the village. Sitting against the wall on the way out is a blind beggar and, as you pass, he asks you for alms. He looks a sorry sight: skinny and sparsely clothed. His eyes are painted with a dark dye to indicate his blindness. You are considering whether to toss him a Gold Piece when an ox cart comes up the road. Seeing you are a stranger, the driver asks you if you would like a lift. Will you accept his offer (turn to **129**) or refuse and instead toss the beggar a Gold Piece (turn to **244**)?

227

Draw your weapon and fight:

MANTICORE   SKILL 12   STAMINA 18

Each time the creature inflicts a wound on you, you must roll one die.
A roll of a 5 or 6 indicates a hit with its scorpion-like tail containing a
poison which will cause 6 STAMINA points' worth of damage unless
you successfully *Test your Luck* (if you are Lucky, the damage will be
normal). If you roll a 1–4, the attack is normal. If you defeat the
creature, turn to **456**.

228

You will have to heave with every ounce of strength in your body to
force the door open. Throw one die three times. If the total thrown is
less than your SKILL score, the door breaks open and you may escape
(turn to **120**) – but you must lose 1 SKILL point. If the total thrown
equals or exceeds your SKILL score, the door will not budge and you
will be trapped in the cave-in unless you can call for help from your
goddess Libra (turn to **160**).

229

One of the merchants has a friend who needs a cesspit in his back yard
filling in and a fresh one digging. This will take you most of the night
to do, but he will feed and pay you. If you wish to take up this offer,
turn to **201**, but if not, you must look for the inn – turn to **134**.

230

You enter the tavern and call to the proprietor. Glandragor himself
comes out. He is a kindly type and is always happy to talk to
strangers. He is also a businessman, and a mug of ale will cost you 2
Gold Pieces. Will you pay up, drink your ale and talk to him (turn to
191) or do you have something for him (turn to **182**)? If you cannot
afford a drink, turn to **92**.

231

Further along the river is another bridge over which the path leads. You cross the bridge and start heading up into the hills. The path winds for some time, taking the gradient leisurely. Suddenly an acorn lands on your head and you hear a tittering coming from the trees above. Looking up you can see tiny figures high in the branches, flying from tree to tree. Another acorn falls, then another. You are being pelted by ELVINS! You may protect yourself with a spell:

ZIP	FOF	WOK	HOP	YAG
359	408	296	382	340

If you do not wish to use a spell, turn to 85.

232

It is now late afternoon. You pass over the brow of the next hill and below you is a village. The path leads into this village and you have little choice but to enter Torrepani.

Torrepani is inhabited by the SVINNS, an aggressive-looking race of man-orcs. But as you enter the village, an air of depression hanging over the place becomes quite apparent. The Svinns take no notice of you and you sit down on a tree stump in the centre of the village surveying the miserable creatures. Will you head for the inn to spend the night (turn to 267) or attempt to make contact with the villagers (turn to 282)?

233

The old man's eyes light up as you produce the axe. 'Where did you get that?' he exclaims. You tell him the story and he takes it from you, overjoyed. Handing you a free mug of ale (you may add 2 STAMINA points for this) he is overwhelmingly grateful and wishes to tell you all he knows to help you. 'First of all,' he says, 'you should visit the Crystal Waterfall. It has great powers of healing and soothing. Here is a pass which will allow you past the guardian (you need not pay if you go). When you leave Birritanti you will reach Kharé through Torrepani. The Svinns live in Torrepani and no doubt their chief will try to persuade you to help find his daughter. She has been carried off by marauders and left as a sacrifice in a dark cave guarded by a deadly Manticore. After Torrepani you will reach Kharé within a day. In fact I am well connected in Kharé. If you have any problems in Kharé, just call for Vik, a friend of mine who has power and influence.' In Kharé,

VIK will be given as a spell option in some encounters. If given such an option, you may choose it to take advantage of Glandragor's connections. Glandragor also offers you a sword – a sturdy but ordinary one – as a replacement weapon and wishes you well as you leave. Add 3 LUCK points for finding Glandragor. You may head for either the Crystal Waterfall (turn to **102**) or the inn (turn to **92**).

234

The gate is open, but you are wary of continuing. This is no normal gate: it stands two or three times the size of any you have seen before. But the only way on is through it, so you continue – though carefully.

To the right, the hill rises sharply upwards and you can see two caves. Will you enter the right-hand cave (turn to **207**), the left-hand cave (turn to **221**) or will you continue past the caves along the path (turn to **82**)?

235

She shouts loudly after you and orders you back. She seems most indignant that you have chosen to ignore her and warns you that you will not go unpunished. Jann is curious and suggests you return to the hut. If you reconsider and see what she wants, turn to **243**. If you continue regardless, turn to **269**.

236

Test your Luck. If you are Lucky, turn to **118**. If you are Unlucky, turn to **223**.

237

You continue up the hill. The climb is steep, but by mid-afternoon you have reached the top. Continuing over the hill, you travel down a gentle slope for the rest of the afternoon. Turn to **220**.

238

Your guess is incorrect. With a wave of the hunchback's hand you feel a sharp pain surge through your body. Lose 2 STAMINA points and 1 LUCK point and return to the junction to take the other path (turn to 38).

239

The door opens on well-oiled hinges and you are in a pitch-black passageway. You may cast a spell if you wish:

SUS	FAR	FIX	BAG	HOW
372	349	422	398	454

Or you may grope down the passageway in the dark (turn to 6). You may decide against this passage and return through the room to the junction (turn to 120).

240

'I have in my house Ragnar's Armband of Swordmastery, which I will gladly give to you if you will free me,' she promises. Will you try to open the cage as she wishes (turn to 4) or doublecross her and search around for it anyway (turn to 213)?

241

If you wish to draw your weapon, turn to 2. If you would rather cast a spell, turn to 275.

242

A short while later, two Head Hunters return and take you from the cage. As they bustle you towards the pot, now steaming as the water heats, you receive a blow on the head. You slump unconscious and never re-awaken. You will provide the natives with fresh meat tonight . . .

243

The old woman invites you into her house and bids you sit down. She is lonely on her own in the woods and appreciates the company of others. Offering you a drink, she shuffles off into the kitchen and returns with two large cups of tea, and one tiny one. Jann is a little suspicious and tells you so. The old woman glares at him and expresses openly her disgust for Minimites. She has forgotten the pot and returns to the kitchen to fetch it. You may, if you wish, switch your cup of tea with hers (turn to **48**) or you may wait for her to return and drink the one she has given you (turn to **146**).

244

You toss him a Gold Piece. 'You are kind, traveller,' the beggar says. Feeling the coin he becomes excited. 'Why, this is a Gold Piece!' he exclaims. 'You are too generous to a poor sightless beggar. Generosity of this sort must not go unrewarded!' Taking a copper key from his pocket he gives it to you, insisting that you take it. 'Years ago I lived in Kharé,' he tells you. 'Kharé was my home and in the cityport I watched over prisoners in the gaol. But Kharé is an evil place, inhabited by all manner of creatures. Beware the Red-Eyes in Kharé or my fate will befall you and you too will have to turn to begging for a living. Kharé is also wary of strangers, but this key will help you should you be captured by the city guards.' The key has a number, 206, stamped into it. You thank the beggar and continue. Turn to **58**.

245

You creep by the sentry post unnoticed. Turn to **237**.

246

As the second day of your journey breaks, you march through the cool morning air of the hills, having now climbed several hundred feet. You reach the brow of a hill and stop in your tracks. To your left is a clearing in which several poles are firmly planted in the ground. Atop the poles are *heads* – some recently fixed, some semi-decayed – human heads, Goblin heads, and one or two heads of creatures you do not recognize, all with sewn-up eyes and mouths. A large X painted on a broad tree is obviously intended as a warning to venture no further. Ahead the path forks to the right and left, but you cannot be sure which path you are warned not to take! Will you continue your climb along the right-hand path (turn to **68**) or take the left-hand path which winds down the side of the hill (turn to **40**)?

247

The skullcap has been stolen from a priest of Daddu-Ley. It has no magical properties of its own but may be useful in spells. Turn to **75**.

248

She hands you a small box. Opening the box you find it contains a miniature vial of glue, a pair of strange-looking nose plugs and four small pebbles – all useful in creating spells. Now turn to **87**.

249

The pipe is made of bamboo and you blow it. It gives off a lively little note. You may take this with you. Turn to **126**.

250

You leave Lea-Ki, the domain of the Hill Giants, and head onwards. It is late afternoon and you may choose either a path running down the hill (turn to **176**) or a path running along the crest of the hill (turn to **188**).

251

The box is empty. But as you look inside, smoke begins to swell up from its depths. The smoke builds up and rises from the box in front of you. Slowly, a face forms in the air; a thin, elf-like face. You watch, transfixed, and suddenly its eyes flick open. Their piercing stare reaches deep into your mind, and you are unable to move. 'Stranger,' the mouth speaks, 'you tamper with forces you know nothing of. I am aware of your quest. You cannot succeed!'

Will you use a spell:

FOG	MAG	RIS	RAN	GAK
455	403	293	377	354

Or will you try to escape from the room (turn to **124**)?

252

Will you fight it with your weapon (turn to **20**) or with a magic spell (turn to **166**)?

253

Your guess is incorrect. With a wave of the hunchback's hand you feel a sharp pain surge through your body. Lose 2 STAMINA points and 1 LUCK point and return to the junction to take the other path (turn to **38**).

254

You race off into the woods in case the commotion attracts any other creatures. For half an hour you run before you stop to rest, when you realize that you are now hopelessly lost. Which direction will you take? Throw one die. If you throw a 1 or a 2, you continue uphill until you reach a path (turn to **68**). If you roll a 3 or 4, you just head in the direction you were travelling (turn to **13**) until you reach a path. If you roll a 5 or 6, you take a downhill course until you reach a well-trodden path (turn to **98**).

255

The door opens. The room inside is dirty and sooty with dust from the mines. It is square, and a door opposite leads onwards. Sitting behind a makeshift desk is a large, filthy GOBLIN who raises his head and sniffs the air as you walk in. His face is black with soot. 'Your smell is strange, intruder!' he challenges. 'You are not permitted here!' Will you prepare to fight him (turn to **47**) or leave as he wishes (turn to **120**)?

256

The creature roars and reaches down to grab you. Unable to avoid it, you feel yourself gripped between its great thumb and forefinger. The pain is excruciating as the creature squeezes but there is nothing you can do. The Giant crushes you to death . . .

257

The inn offers hot meals for sale and if you wish to stop and eat the charge will be 1 Gold Piece. Bread and goat's cheese are also available if you wish to buy food to take with you, and the price of two meals' worth is 2 Gold Pieces. If you wish to sit down and eat, turn to **116**. If you wish to buy Provisions, do so and pay the 2 Gold Pieces. Or, if you wish to continue with or without new Provisions, turn to **131**.

258

You flip open the top of the box and jump back quickly. Inside the box are 5 Gold Pieces and a key, but these are guarded by a vicious SCORPION. You may try if you wish to grab either the Gold Pieces or the key – but only one item at a time (i.e. Gold Pieces one by one). Each time you attempt a grab, *Test your Luck*. If you are Lucky, you succeed in grabbing an object. If you are Unlucky, you are stung by the Scorpion and must lose *half* your STAMINA (round *down* any odd STAMINA points). When you are finished with this box, turn to **199** if you took the key. Otherwise you may either try the other box (turn to **251**) or leave the village (turn to **196**).

259

You manage to avoid the Goblins and sneak off along a downhill path into the woods. Turn to **202**.

260

You are forced upwards against the ceiling as the water level rises. But Libra has not deserted you and an air pocket forms around your head. As you thrash about in the water, you are able to breathe easily and soon you relax, knowing you are safe. After several minutes, the water drains off, leaving you on the ground unharmed, although somewhat damp. The sealing wall disappears into the floor and you return to the large chamber to choose another passage. Will you take the right-hand path (turn to **3**) or the left-hand path (turn to **16**)?

261

As you unstrap the pack, one of the bandits grabs it from your hands while the other leaps at you and clouts you with the hilt of his sword. You fall to the ground dazed and the bandits make off with your belongings. Lose 2 STAMINA points. You have now lost anything you were carrying in the backpack including gold and Provisions (but not your sword). Eventually you pick yourself up and continue your journey. Turn to **131**.

262

You are correct. The hunchback stands aside to let you pass. As you start across the bridge he wishes you well on your way. You march swiftly across in case he may have some other trap in store. But instead he calls out a clue which may be useful in the journey ahead.

He is a sly old creature and you must be careful to mark his words well:

> *'Beware the lair of the cave-demon's maze.*
> *For traps as deadly as Medusa's gaze*
> *Greet travellers who, of luck bereft,*
> *Take passageways not to the left.'*

You consider these words as you cross the valley. You may add 2 LUCK points for your success. On the other side of the bridge you follow the path over the hill and down the other side. It is now late afternoon. Turn to **220**.

263

You finish the job well and in good time and the villager pays you 3 Gold Pieces. You leave Dhumpus in the early morning light. Turn to **208**.

264

He grunts and motions for you to follow, taking you through the village to a large hut. Inside, you discover that the building is evidently a storage house and a quartermaster, somewhat plumper than your guide, is seated at a table. The villager explains you wish to do business and leaves you with the fat man, who bids you take a seat. The merchant has the following items for sale. If you are interested in any of them, turn to the reference indicated:

A herbalist's potion	Turn to **107**
A fine-edged broadsword	Turn to **214**
A musical pipe	Turn to **22**
An axe with strange carvings	Turn to **141**
A bag containing teeth	Turn to **5**
A fine, glittering jewel	Turn to **60**

If none of these interest you, turn to **163**.

265

Exhausted from the battle, you examine the Giant and its domain as you recover your breath. A pouch around its waist contains 8 Gold Pieces. You may also take any part of the creature that you think may be useful. A large loaf in the cave is too large for you to carry, but you may eat from it if you wish (turn to **284**). Otherwise turn to **250**.

266

You find an ale-house and walk in. Gruff voices come from inside but, when you enter, the drinkers watch you suspiciously and the noise subsides. Several Hill Dwellers sit around a table. The owner of the house tells you that you are in the village of Kristatanti and that a mug of ale will cost you 1 Gold Piece. If you cannot afford this price you will have to leave the ale-house (turn to **62**). Otherwise you may pay him, take your drink and sit down at the table next to an old, wrinkled man (turn to **192**) or a younger man with sharp features (turn to **96**).

267

The inn serves hot food for 3 Gold Pieces and you may eat here if you can afford it. If you have not yet eaten today, add 2 STAMINA points if you buy a meal (1 STAMINA point if you have already eaten). A bed for the night costs 5 Gold Pieces. If you will sleep here, turn to 8. If you would rather leave the village and sleep rough, turn to **35**.

268

The door is locked. You may try charging the door down (turn to **93**) or you may cast a spell:

DOM	PAP	HUF	HOW	DOP
351	311	374	449	291

269

Now screaming at you, she calls loudly into the air. A cracking to your left makes you wheel round, just in time to see a tree swaying as its trunk splits and it falls towards you. *Test your Luck*. If you are Lucky, you spring aside just before it topples on you. If you are Unlucky, you are too late and the tree lands on you, crushing you and your miniature companion to death. If you survive, turn to **276**.

270

The bees swarm around you but you are powerless to defend yourself as you must use your hands to grip the tree. Throw one die. If you throw a 1–4, then this is the number of STAMINA points you lose as the bees sting you. If you roll a 5 or 6, you are lucky and avoid being stung. When you reach the hive, you knock it down to the ground.

Cutting open the hive on the ground, you may take with you the wax and the honey. The honey will provide you with enough nourishment for one meal. Turn to **9**.

271

You try knocking on another door. This time a voice calls 'Who is it?' and you enter. Turn to **158**.

272

As you bite into your bread, a sharp pain in your leg makes you swing round. In a tree a short distance away, you can see the black face of a HEAD HUNTER leering at you as it lowers a blowpipe. You become dizzy and pass out as the poison takes effect. Your head will soon be joining the others on a pole at the last junction . . .

273

Before your eyes the snakes form a living ladder, stretching back up to the passage above! When it is formed, you may climb back up and return to the main chamber, where you may take either the right-hand (turn to **3**) or the left-hand passage (turn to **16**). Remember that you cannot call on Libra again now.

274

You open the stopper on the bottle of potion and take a sniff. Phew! The pungent odour of Blimberry juice hits your nostrils. Blimberry is a strange fruit which ordinarily would never be eaten by humans or animals (having such a foul smell). But its medicinal properties have been discovered by all species and it appears to be nature's healer. You may take this potion at any time, except in battle, to restore 3 STAMINA points. Or you may use the potion in sorcery. There is enough in the bottle for one dose. Turn to **126**.

275

You snatch your arm back against the pull and, as you do so, a shape begins to form in front of you. You are now facing a large, two-tailed SERPENT which hisses menacingly at you. One of its tails is wrapped around your arm. Which spell will you use?

KIL	SUN	GOP	LAW	HOW
314	404	334	355	426

If you cannot, or choose not to, use any of these, you will have to arm yourself. Turn to **2**.

276

As you pick yourself up, the old woman suddenly appears in front of you. 'You may not ignore the invitation of Gaza Moon!' she says, and she points a finger at you. A blue crackle from her hand takes you unawares as a lightning blast flies towards you. Will you defend yourself with a spell:

If you are a warrior you have no escape from the blast.

ZIP	GUM	LAM	FIL	SUS
322	434	418	304	392

If you know none of these, the blast hits you and charred remains are all that are left of you. The Sorceress Gaza Moon must not be ignored . . .

277

The fall is not too far, but there is a chance of injury. Throw two dice and compare the total with your LUCK score. If the total is *less than* your LUCK, you are unhurt. If the total *equals* your LUCK, deduct 1 STAMINA point for minor bruising. If the total *exceeds* your LUCK, deduct 3 STAMINA points as you have badly twisted your arm. If you throw a *double six*, then you have landed on your head, breaking your neck in the fall and your adventure ends here. Turn to **110** if you did not die.

278

You follow the path back up to the junction and continue towards Dhumpus. Turn to **54**.

279

When you awake, you find yourself inside a hut with your hands bound. Seeing you stir, a creature by the door jumps to its feet. In fact it jumps *above* its feet and now hovers attentively in the air, watching you. Your guard is man-like but short and thin. You have been captured by ELVINS!

Elvins are impish creatures, more mischievous than malevolent. They love pranks and practical jokes. Soon several have gathered in your room. They ask whether you are a magician and, if so, will you show them some tricks. If you will perform for them, turn to **132**. Otherwise turn to **218**.

280

If you have investigated only one or two of his offerings, you may choose another from the list below. But if you have considered three artefacts already, you may not try a fourth and you must leave the merchant – turn to **91**.

The herbalist's potion	Turn to **107**
The broadsword	Turn to **214**
The musical pipe	Turn to **22**
The axe	Turn to **141**
The bag of teeth	Turn to **5**
The jewel	Turn to **60**

281

Test your Luck. If you are Lucky, they do not notice you – you go back to sleep and set off again at sunrise (turn to **148**). If you are Unlucky, one of them sees you across the stream and points you out to the others – turn to **12**.

282

You approach a group of Svinns deep in conversation and take a seat with them. They are discussing a friend, apparently killed in the night by an assassin's blade. Gradually you work your way into the conversation and you soon learn the reason for the depression which hangs over the village. The village chief's daughter has been captured by a band of marauders and offered as a sacrifice to a powerful cave demon. According to an ancient prophecy, a dreadful scourge will overrun the village if the chief's line ever ends – and his daughter is the chief's only heir.

You tell them of your own travels and the creatures you have met. They realize you are a truly heroic adventurer and become very interested in you. Suddenly one springs at you while another runs off into the village. You are held fast in a vice-like grip, but as you struggle more Svinns arrive. They march you off to a hut at the edge of the village. Turn to **71**.

283

You settle down to make camp for the night. You may take Provisions here and, if you do so, you may add 2 STAMINA points if you have not yet eaten since leaving Analand, or 1 STAMINA point if you have already eaten on your journey. You may only eat if you have Provisions with you. As you curl up in your blanket to sleep, there is a chance that you may encounter a wandering night creature. *Remember this reference* (as you will return here afterwards) and turn to **123**. Night creatures are less likely to approach you in your camp, so you may add 2 points to the die roll you will be required to make.

After your night's sleep you may add either 2 STAMINA points, if you encountered no night creatures, or 1 STAMINA point if your sleep was disturbed. Then you set off along the trail. Turn to **31**.

284

The loaf is not particularly pleasant, but is fairly nourishing. You may make a meal of it and restore 2 STAMINA points. Then turn to **250**.

285

You may either fight the Ogre with your weapon:

OGRE	SKILL 8		STAMINA 7

If you win, turn to **15**. Alternatively you may cast a spell:

WOK	WAL	KIL	DIM	ROK
400	352	331	375	312

286

As you have no doubt already learned, Jann will not leave you. And while he is with you, your magic will not work. You may not use any spells until you rid yourself of this little pest. Now turn to **197**.

287

Deduct 5 STAMINA points. There is no such spell as this. Return to **87** and choose again.

288

Deduct 4 STAMINA points. Your spell creates an invisible force field around you. Try as they may, the Bandits cannot harm you or even get close to you. Realizing the power of your sorcery, they run back into the village, allowing you to continue. Turn to **131**.

289

Deduct 5 STAMINA points. There is no such spell as this. Return to **47** and choose again.

290

Deduct 5 STAMINA points. There is no such spell as this. You fall down into the pit. Turn to **277**.

291

Deduct 2 STAMINA points. The door shudders and the handle turns. On your guard, you watch as it opens, allowing you into the room inside. Turn to **39**.

292

Deduct 2 STAMINA points. You concentrate and slowly focus your mind on a large rock in the corner of the hut. Before their eyes, this rock turns into a glittering pile of treasure. They gasp, as they can see jewels, gold, silver and gems forming from nothing. They chatter excitedly and nod towards you, smiling happily. One of them ventures over to touch the treasure and, as he does so, you release the spell. The Elvins are impressed with your trick and return your backpack, soon allowing you to leave the village. Turn to **196**.

293

Deduct 5 STAMINA points. There is no such spell as this, and the spirit laughs as you try to cast it. Turn to **124**.

294

Deduct 5 STAMINA points. There is no such spell as this. Return to **203** and choose again.

295

Deduct 2 STAMINA points. You cast your spell and, with a flash, five replicas of yourself appear in front of the creature. It chooses one of these images to attack. Choose which of the images is the real you by noting down a number between one and six. Then roll one die to determine which image the creature goes for. If you roll the same number as you have chosen for yourself, it has been lucky and selected the real you! Turn to **20** to resolve the combat. If it does not choose the real you, you may escape from it and continue. Turn to **193**.

296

Deduct 1 STAMINA point. Do you have a Gold Piece with you? If not, your spell will not work – turn to **85**. If you have a Gold Piece, you place it on your wrist and cast your spell. An invisible shield forms around it, large enough for you to hide behind. You are able to pass safely through the hail of acorns – but you lose your Gold Piece. Turn to **7**.

297

Deduct 4 STAMINA points. You hold up your hand and cast the spell. A small burning fireball materializes in your palm and you fling it at the Wood Golem. The creature catches fire immediately and shrieks loudly. Alianna runs off for water to douse the fire before her house goes up, and you make a hasty exit. Turn to **169**.

298

Deduct 2 STAMINA points. You cast your spell and wait for it to take effect. Almost immediately, you start to expand. Your whole body begins to grow until you are almost three times your normal size. This allows you to finish the job quite quickly and you manage to get half a night's sleep. Add 2 STAMINA points, then turn to **263**.

299

Deduct 1 STAMINA point. Do you have any Blimberry juice with you? If not, you must return to **158** and choose again. If you can cast the spell over Blimberry juice, you do so and sprinkle the enchanted juice on to the villagers. At first this appears to burn them, but then the healing potion takes effect. This is a *plague village*; everyone in it has plague. You have just healed this family and they are on their knees, thanking you. You talk to them for some time and they give you one important warning: Beware the Black Lotus Flower. Eventually you leave. Turn to **220**.

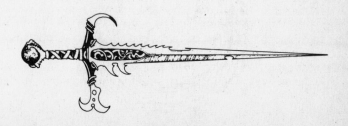

300

Deduct 1 STAMINA point. You cast the spell but nothing happens. Return to **220** and choose again.

301

Deduct 1 STAMINA point. You cannot use this spell as you do not have the Gold-Backed Mirror it requires. Draw your weapon and turn to **227**.

302

Deduct 1 STAMINA point. The creature advances and you cast your spell. You panic as nothing happens! You cannot use this spell as you do not have the Potion of Fire Water it requires. The Manticore whips round its tail and, although you try your best to evade it, the sting grazes your arm. Deduct 6 STAMINA points. If you will now draw your weapon and fight, turn to **227**. If you would prefer to cast another spell, turn to **364**.

303

Deduct 1 STAMINA point. Do you have any small pebbles with you? If not, you must return to **63** and choose again quickly. If you have any small pebbles, you cast the spell on them and toss them at the snakes. They explode on impact, killing several of the snakes and frightening the others. You throw three such missiles and have given yourself some breathing space. However, on consideration, there seems to be no way you can escape from the pit unless you are able to call on Libra. If you have not yet used her help, turn to **273**. Otherwise there is little you can do. Your journey has ended here . . .

304

Deduct 5 STAMINA points. You cast your spell but nothing happens. The blast hits you in the chest, killing you instantly. Your journey ends here . . .

305

Deduct 4 STAMINA points. You cast your spell and wait for the lightning bolt to shoot at the assassin. But nothing happens! The Minimite screams at you, 'Don't waste your time on spells. Minimites are protected – though it is sometimes a curse – with a protection aura. You cannot cast spells when I am about!' You must return to 117 and fight the assassin.

306

Deduct 4 STAMINA points. You cast the spell – but nothing happens! The little creature chuckles. 'You are wasting your time with magic while I'm around,' it laughs. Turn to 171.

307

As you try desperately to make your spell work, the creature pounces. Its huge weight lands on you and its claws rip your clothes. That deadly sting comes over at you, but you are powerless to defend yourself. It pierces your chest. Shortly the poison will take effect. You have failed in your mission . . .

308

Deduct 1 STAMINA point. Do you have a bamboo flute with you? If not, you should not be at this reference and must deduct a further 3 STAMINA points as the Bandits attack and turn back to **104**. If you have such a flute, you may take it from your bag, cast your spell and play. The angry faces of the Bandits turn to expressions of astonishment as they find their limbs jerking in time to the music, quite out of control. They drop their swords and are soon dancing merrily before you. Piping loudly, you direct them back to the village and, as they dance off, you continue your journey. Turn to **131**.

309

Deduct 1 STAMINA point. You cast the spell unsuccessfully, as you do not have the skullcap it requires. The Goblin seizes its chance and attacks you fiercely. Deduct another 3 STAMINA points and return to **47** to choose again.

310

Deduct 5 STAMINA points. There is no such spell as this. Return to **66** and choose again. But hurry!

311

Deduct 5 STAMINA points. There is no such spell as this. Return to **268** and choose again.

312

Deduct 1 STAMINA point. You cannot use this spell as you do not have the stone dust it requires. The Ogre swings its fist and knocks you back against a wall. Deduct another 2 STAMINA points, return to **285** and choose again.

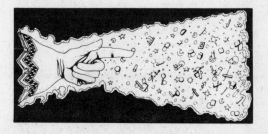

313

Deduct 5 STAMINA points. You have chosen a non-existent spell. Return to **166** and choose again.

314

Deduct 5 STAMINA points. There is no such spell as this. Return to **275** and choose again.

315

Deduct 5 STAMINA points. There is no such spell as this. Return to **74** and choose again.

316

Deduct 2 STAMINA points as you cast the spell. You cast it, not over yourself, but over one of the Elvins who seems to be in charge. The others stand agog as he suddenly duplicates until six replicas stand in front of them! The leader laughs – or rather all six of them laugh together – and the sight is most amusing. Soon all the Elvins are laughing and the leader and his replicas hold out their hands to shake with their comrades. Five of the other Elvins, of course, grasp thin air. The spell soon wears off and the creatures congratulate you, returning your backpack and allowing you to leave the village. Turn to **196**.

317

Deduct 4 STAMINA points. You cast the spell and the creature looks confused. It steps forwards and kicks the staff of the halberd, knocking it out of its hands. Cursing, it picks the weapon up, merely to drop it again! You may seize your chance and attack. While under the effect of the spell, the Troll will fight at:

TROLL SENTRY   SKILL 4   STAMINA 7

The spell will last for 4 Attack Rounds and will then wear off. Before each Attack Round after the fourth, roll one die. If the number is odd, the Troll cannot regain his halberd and will continue fighting with a SKILL of 4. If you roll an even number, it will regain its weapon and fight with a SKILL of 8. Turn to **177** if you win.

318

Deduct 4 STAMINA points. You cast the spell and point your finger at the hole. With a flash, a burst of lightning flies from your fingertip and blasts the ground. Earth flies all around and, as you see when the air clears, you have created a fine hole, a little rough around the edges, but nevertheless you have saved yourself a lot of work. You settle down to sleep for the rest of the night. You may recover the 3 STAMINA points you would have lost for missing a night's sleep. Turn to **263**.

319

Deduct 1 STAMINA point. You cast the spell and wait for something to happen, but nothing does. You do not have a Giant's tooth which you may cast this spell on. Turn to **256**.

320

Deduct 5 STAMINA points. There is no such spell as this. Return to **4** and choose again.

321

Deduct 2 STAMINA points. You cast your spell, but nothing happens! The Minimite tells you not to waste your energy on spells while he is around. Will you continue (turn to **73**) or return and take the other path (turn to **51**)?

322

Deduct 5 STAMINA points. You cast your spell but nothing happens. Unable to defend yourself, the blast hits you in the chest. You cry out in pain and drop to the ground. Your journey has ended here . . .

323

Deduct 4 STAMINA points. You cast your spell just in time, and your invisible wall blocks off the passage. The great boulder hits it with some considerable force, causing the whole cave to shake. It bounces off your barrier and rolls back up the slope. You must now continue either by returning to the last junction and taking the other fork (turn to 63) or by returning to the main chamber and taking the other passage (turn to 16).

324

Deduct 1 STAMINA point. You cannot use this spell as you do not have the Galehorn it requires. Turn to 64.

325

Deduct 2 STAMINA points. The creature makes a half turn and prepares to swing its stinging tail at you. But as you cast the spell, it pauses briefly and shakes its head, as if something has hit it. Its movements become slow and you may now seize your chance to either attack it with your weapon (turn to 227) or cast an attacking spell (turn to 364). If you choose to attack, it will fight at half SKILL for the first 4 Attack Rounds.

326

Deduct 5 STAMINA points. There is no such spell as this. Turn to 307.

327

There is no such spell as this. Deduct 5 points from your STAMINA and return to 104.

328

Deduct 1 STAMINA point. Do you have any beeswax with you? If not, you must deduct 3 extra STAMINA points as the Goblin attacks and return to 47. If you do have beeswax, you may rub it on your sword and return to 47. Fight the Goblin as normal, but you may double any damage you inflict on the Goblin while your sword has been magically sharpened. The effect will only last for this fight, and you have used up half your beeswax.

329

Deduct 1 STAMINA point. You try in vain to cast the spell as you do not have the Galehorn it requires. As you recite your spell again and again, the ceiling collapses entirely. There is nothing you can do as you are buried for ever in the rubble . . .

330

Deduct 1 STAMINA point. Your spell will not work as you do not possess the Jewel-Studded Medallion you need to complete it. You fall down into the pit. Turn to 277, where you will be required to make a dice roll. Since you have been fumbling unsuccessfully with your spell, you must add 3 points to the dice roll.

331

Deduct 5 STAMINA points. There is no such spell as this. Return to 285 and choose again.

332

Deduct 1 STAMINA point. You cast the spell but nothing happens. You cannot use this spell as you do not have the Brass Pendulum it requires. You must draw your weapon and fight. Turn to 20.

333
Deduct 4 STAMINA points. Your spell is, however, ineffective. You cannot cast spells when your hands are bound! You have wasted your efforts. Turn to **112**.

334
Deduct 5 STAMINA points. There is no such spell as this. Return to **275** and choose again.

335
Deduct 4 STAMINA points. You cast the spell quickly and point towards the beast. A lightning blast shoots from your fingertip and catches the Wolfhound square in the forehead. It drops to the ground, dead. Turn to **50**.

336
Deduct 5 STAMINA points. You cast the spell but nothing happens. Turn back to **220** and choose again.

337
Deduct 5 STAMINA points. There is no such spell as this. Return to **158** and choose again.

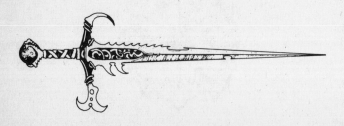

338

Deduct 4 STAMINA points. You cast the spell and the club drops out of the Giant's hand. It grunts and reaches down to retrieve it. Taking another step, it again drops the club. Your spell is working! Twice more it does this until it eventually leaves the club on the floor and attacks you with its bare hands. You will have to fight it, but without its weapon:

HILL GIANT   SKILL 6   STAMINA 11

If you win, turn to **265**.

339

Deduct 1 STAMINA point. Do you have a Bamboo Flute with you? If not, the Wood Golem attacks for 2 STAMINA points' worth of damage – return to **87** and choose again. If you have a Bamboo Pipe, you pull it out of your backpack, cast your spell and play. The Golem stops and looks at you strangely. Its shoulders shrug and it shivers. It looks around and one leg starts twitching on the floor. Uncontrollably it takes a little leap forward, then hops back, landing neatly on its toes. It cannot understand what is happening! The bulky creature is doing a little dance in front of you! You keep it occupied while you back off towards the door. Turn to **169**.

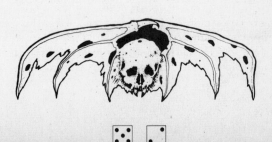

340

Deduct 5 STAMINA points. There is no such spell as this. Return to **231** and choose again.

341

Deduct 5 STAMINA points. You cast your spell but nothing happens. Will you continue (turn to **73**) or return and take the other path (turn to **51**)?

342

Deduct 1 STAMINA point. You cast the spell but nothing happens. Return to **117** and choose again.

343

Deduct 1 STAMINA point. Unfortunately, you do not have the Staff of Oak Sapling that this spell requires and your poor choice has left you no time to plan an alternative escape. The great boulder rolls over you, crushing you on to the floor. Your journey has ended here . . .

344

Deduct 5 STAMINA points. There is no such spell as this and, as you try to make it work, the snakes are upon you. This is the end of your journey . . .

345

Deduct 5 STAMINA points. There is no such spell as this and, while you have been trying unsuccessfully to cast it, the creature whips its tail round to sting you. You fall to the floor to avoid it. Will you now attack it with your weapon (turn to **227**) or will you cast another spell (turn to **364**)?

346

Deduct 4 STAMINA points. Your spell creates a large fireball in your hand, which you fling at the beast. It hits the Manticore in the side and the creature roars out in pain. You may turn to 420 to finish it off.

347

Deduct 1 STAMINA point. You cannot choose this spell as you do not have the Ring of Green Metal it requires. Turn to 307.

348

Deduct 4 STAMINA points. You cast your spell and wait. The Bandits pause, expecting something to happen . . . but nothing does! This spell works only on non-intelligent creatures. The Bandits leap at you and one gashes your arm with his sword, inflicting 2 STAMINA points of damage. Return to 104 either to cast another spell or to draw your weapon.

349

Deduct 1 STAMINA point. You cannot cast this spell as you do not have the Orb of Crystal it requires. Deduct a further 2 STAMINA points as you try without success to make the spell work. Return to 239 and choose again.

350

Deduct 5 STAMINA points. There is no such spell as this. Return to 66 and choose again.

351

Deduct 5 STAMINA points. There is no such spell as this. Return to 268 and choose again.

352

Deduct 4 STAMINA points. You cast the spell and, as the Ogre leaps to attack, it collides with something solid. You have stopped it with your invisible wall. You may now escape from the room while holding the Ogre at bay. On your way out you may grab a gem from the table – the Ogre's job was to grind the rocks mined from the mine into such gems. This gem is worth 10 Gold Pieces. You may use it to buy things and barter, but you will not be given change, no matter how little your purchase costs. Turn to 144.

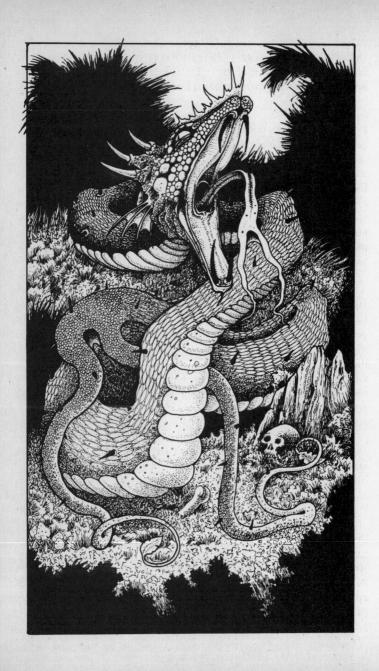

353
Deduct 1 STAMINA point. You try the spell, but nothing happens as you do not have the Bracelet of Bone it requires. The Elvins are not impressed and quickly bind your hands again – only this time tighter, causing you some pain and the loss of another STAMINA point. Turn to **218**.

354
Deduct 1 STAMINA point. 'Fool,' calls out the Spirit, 'I know that spell well. Do you not have the Black Facemask that it requires?' You do not have the mask and, in panic, you try to leave the hut. Turn to **124**.

355
Deduct 4 STAMINA points. Holding your hands up, you command the serpent to release you. It does so and backs off into the bushes. You watch it retreat until it slowly vanishes from sight. Turn to **137**.

356
Deduct 2 STAMINA points. You cast the spell and immediately begin to grow larger. Within moments you stand three times your normal size. The Elvin looks on with awe and hesitates, not sure whether to fight or fly. You may either attack it or *Test your Luck*. If you are Lucky, the creature will fly off, its companions following it into the woods and allowing you to settle back down to sleep. You awake at sunrise – turn to **148**. If you are Unlucky, the Elvin will continue its battle. If you end up fighting the creature, return to **203** and have your battle, but because of your size you may double your SKILL score.

357
Deduct 5 STAMINA points. There is no such spell as this. In fact you discover that you are unable to cast a spell anyway, as your hands are bound (remember this in future). Turn to **112**.

358
Deduct 1 STAMINA point. You cannot cast this spell as you do not have the Green-Haired Wig it requires. The Goblins spring at you and attack. Lose 2 STAMINA points as the first Goblin slashes at you. Return to **217** but you may not choose another spell; you must draw your weapon and fight them.

359

Deduct 1 STAMINA point. You cast the spell and wait. Nothing happens. You cannot use this spell as you do not have the Ring of Green Metal it requires. Turn to **85**.

360

Deduct 1 STAMINA point. Do you have any beeswax with you? If not, you may not cast this spell – return to **4** and choose again. If you have beeswax, you may wipe it on to your weapon to enhance its effect. Turn to **142** and try smashing the lock. But you may deduct 2 points from the dice roll you make against SKILL and, if you succeed in smashing the lock *on your first attempt*, you need not lose the SKILL penalty.

361

Deduct 1 STAMINA point. Do you have a Giant's tooth? If not, turn to **256**. If you have found one on your travels, you drop it on the floor and cast your spell on it. The great creature watches inquisitively, then you both jump back as a plume of smoke rises into the air. Out of the smoke steps another Giant, though this one will do your bidding. You command him to fight:

HILL GIANT	SKILL 9	STAMINA 11
MAGICAL GIANT	SKILL 8	STAMINA 9

Resolve this battle. If the Hill Giant defeats your champion, you will have to finish the battle off yourself. If your Giant wins, he will then disappear and you may turn to **265**.

362

Deduct 1 STAMINA point. You cannot use this spell as you do not have the Potion of Fire Water it requires. Return to **201** and choose again.

363

Deduct 1 STAMINA point. You cannot use this spell as you do not have the Sun Jewel it requires. As you try to get it to work, the Troll leaps and slashes at your leg, causing 2 STAMINA points' worth of damage. Return to 99, but you must now fight the Troll.

364

As the Manticore turns to face you, you may cast an attacking spell:

YOB	KIN	HOT	GOB	KIL
388	301	346	369	395

If you know none of these, draw your weapon and turn to 227.

365

Deduct 4 STAMINA points. You cast your spell and an invisible force field forms itself around you, sealing you into a pocket of air. Although the water floods around you, you are quite safe. After several moments, the sealing wall lowers and the water drains off. You may continue by either returning to the junction and taking the other fork (turn to 151) or going back to the main chamber and taking the other passageway (turn to 3).

366

Deduct 1 STAMINA point. You cannot use this spell as you do not have the Jewel-Studded Medallion it requires. While you are trying to cast it, the snakes have taken an interest in you. Roll one die. This is the number of STAMINA points that you lose when they bite you. If you roll a six, one of the bites has been poisonous and you must *Test your Luck* – if you are Lucky, you survive; if you are Unlucky, you die from the poison. If you are still alive, return to 63 and choose again.

367

Deduct 1 STAMINA point. Do you have a vial of glue with you? If not you must think of another means of escape (turn to 83). If you have some glue, you cast your spell and fling the vial at the passage floor in front of the boulder. Sweating with anxiety, you breathe a sigh of relief as the huge rock rolls on to the glue and holds fast. The whole area shakes with the tremendous strain. You may now either go back to the junction in the passage and take the other fork (turn to 63) or return to the main chamber and take the other passage (turn to 16).

368

Deduct 5 STAMINA points. You cast the spell and wait for something to happen, but nothing does. Return to **117** and choose again.

369

Do you have any Goblins' teeth with you? If so you may throw as many as you wish on to the ground and cast your spell. Deduct 1 STAMINA point per tooth. With a cloud of smoke, this number of Goblins now stand before you and you may command them to attack the Manticore. Resolve the battle (the Goblins will attack one after the other):

MANTICORE	SKILL 12	STAMINA 18
GOBLINS	SKILL 5	STAMINA 5

Each time the Manticore hits a Goblin, roll one die. On a roll of 5 or 6, it will have stung with its poisonous tail, killing the Goblin. 1–4 is a normal hit. If your Goblins win, turn to **456**. If the Manticore defeats all your Goblins, you may either finish the job with your sword (turn to **227**) or cast another spell (turn to **420**).

370

Deduct 5 STAMINA points. There is no such spell as this. Turn to **307**.

371

Deduct 1 STAMINA point. You have chosen a spell you are not able to use as you do not have the Pearl Ring it requires. Lose another 3 STAMINA points as the Bandits attack and return to **104** to make another choice.

372

Deduct 2 STAMINA points. You cast your spell and begin to get a strong feeling that there is danger ahead. A voice inside tells you not to go this way. Will you heed this warning and return to the junction or continue regardless? If you wish to continue, turn to **6**. If you will turn back, turn to **120**.

373

Deduct 2 STAMINA points. You cast the spell and wait anxiously. The huge door creaks on its hinges and slowly opens, just in time for you to nip through before the ceiling collapses! Turn to **120**.

374

Deduct 1 STAMINA point. This spell will not work as you do not have the Galehorn it requires. Return to **268** to try another choice.

375

Deduct 2 STAMINA points. You cast the spell and wait for it to take effect. The Ogre lunges at you but suddenly stops and shakes its head, looking at itself, then at you, with a puzzled expression. It takes a step forward, then grunts and steps backwards, thoroughly confused. You may either fight it now in its incapacitated state (it will fight with a SKILL of 4 and a STAMINA of 7) and, if you win, turn to **15**. Alternatively you may leave the room (turn to **144**).

376

Deduct 5 STAMINA points. There is no such spell as this and the Elvins are not impressed as you unsuccessfully try to cast it. They bind your hands again, only this time tighter, causing you some pain. Turn to **218**.

377

Deduct 5 STAMINA points. There is no such spell as this, and the Spirit laughs as you try to cast it. Turn to **124**.

378

Deduct 1 STAMINA point. You cannot use this spell as you do not have the Pearl Ring it requires. While you are trying to get it to work, the Elvin sweeps in and attacks again. Deduct another 3 STAMINA points. Return to **203** and choose again.

379

Deduct 5 STAMINA points. There is no such spell as this. In fact you may not cast a spell anyway, as your hands are bound (remember this in future). Turn to 112.

380

Deduct 4 STAMINA points. You cast your spell and hold your hands in the air. You command it to hold its ground. It is not too happy with you, but does not move and you are able to step round it. Turn to 118.

381

Deduct 5 STAMINA points. There is no such spell as this. Return to 217 and choose again.

382

Deduct 5 STAMINA points. There is no such spell as this. Return to 231 and choose again.

383

Deduct 2 STAMINA points. You cast the spell and the creature stops. It takes a step forward but its actions have become sluggish under your spell. Return to 87 and fight it; for the first four Attack Rounds, the Wood Golem will fight with a SKILL of 4.

384

Deduct 1 STAMINA point. You cast the spell and wait for something to happen. Nothing does. You cannot use this spell without the Pearl Ring it requires. The Hill Giant watches you, then swings its club, clipping your side as you spring backwards. Lose 2 STAMINA points and turn to 256.

385

Deduct 1 STAMINA point. You cannot use this spell as you do not have the Black Facemask it requires. Return to 158 and choose again.

386

Deduct 1 STAMINA point. Do you have a Gold Piece with you? If not, return to 99 and choose again. If you do have such a coin, you place it on your wrist and cast your spell. The coin sticks and you can feel an invisible shield bound to your wrist. You may now fight the Troll Sentry with extra defence:

TROLL SENTRY   SKILL 8   STAMINA 7

Because of your shield, you may deduct 2 from the Troll's throw on Attack Strength. If you win, turn to 177. After the fight, you must lose the Gold Piece, which becomes useless metal.

387

Deduct 2 STAMINA points. You cast your spell – but nothing happens! You are puzzling this out, when the little creature chuckles. 'You are wasting your time using your magic while I'm around!' it says. Turn to 171.

388

Deduct 1 STAMINA point. Do you have a Giant's tooth with you? If not, you cannot cast this spell and must turn to 227 to defend yourself with your weapon. If you do have a Giant's tooth, you place it on the floor and cast your spell. A cloud of smoke appears around the tooth and, as it clears, a large Giant stands in its place! You command the Giant to attack the Manticore and it turns towards the startled beast. Resolve this battle:

MANTICORE   SKILL 12   STAMINA 18
GIANT   SKILL 8   STAMINA 9

Each time the Manticore hits the Giant, you must roll one die. A roll of 5 or 6 indicates a hit with the sting in its tail, which is poisonous, and will do 6 STAMINA points' worth of damage. A roll of 1–4 indicates normal damage. If your Giant wins, turn to 456. If the Manticore wins, you may either finish the job off yourself (turn to 227) or cast another spell (turn to 420).

389

Deduct 5 STAMINA points. There is no such spell as this, so nothing happens. You duck quickly as it swings its deadly tail round and tries to sting you. If you now wish to draw your weapon and fight, turn to **227**. If you wish to cast another spell, turn to **364**.

390

Deduct 2 STAMINA points. You cast the spell and wait. From some-where inside, a voice warns you that the situation is not good. Your only hope is to empty your backpack, open it out to fill with air, and hold it tightly over your face up to the ceiling. This you do. *Test your Luck*. If you are Lucky, you manage to trap sufficient air to save you before the deluge fills the room. If you are Unlucky, you lose hold of the bag and must try another method of escape (turn to **64**). If you were Lucky, the water eventually drains when the wall behind you lowers. You may return to the junction and take the other fork (turn to **151**) or go back to the main chamber and take the other passageway (turn to **3**). You may collect your belongings from the floor, but anything that would have been spoiled by the water (e.g. Provisions) is now lost for ever.

391

Deduct 5 STAMINA points. There is no such spell as this. You have now left yourself no time to plan an alternative escape and, in a flash, the boulder is on you, crushing you beneath it. Your journey has ended here . . .

392

Deduct 2 STAMINA points. You cast your spell but nothing happens. The Minimite shrieks, cursing himself. He is protected from magic with an anti-magic aura, and most spells will not work in his pres-ence. Unfortunately it is a little too late to learn this, as the lightning blast hits you. Your journey ends here . . .

393
Deduct 5 STAMINA points. You cast the spell but nothing happens. Return to **117** and choose again.

394
Deduct 2 STAMINA points. You cast your spell, but nothing happens! The Minimite tells you not to waste your energy on spells while he is around. Will you continue (turn to **73**) or return and take the other path (turn to **51**)?

395
Deduct 5 STAMINA points. There is no such spell as this. Return to **364** and choose again.

396
Deduct 5 STAMINA points. There is no such spell as this. Return to **123** and choose again.

397
Deduct 5 STAMINA points. There is no such spell as this. Return to **47** and choose again.

398
Deduct 5 STAMINA points. There is no such spell as this. Return to **239** and choose again.

399
Deduct 2 STAMINA points. Your fall is broken and you float gently down to the ground below, landing softly on your knees. Turn to **110**.

400

Deduct 1 STAMINA point. Do you have a Gold Piece with you? If not, deduct 2 extra STAMINA points when the Ogre leaps at you and attacks while you fumble with your spell (return to **285**). If you do have a coin, you place it on your wrist and cast the spell. You can feel an invisible shield fixed to your wrist and you may now fight the Ogre at an advantage. Turn back to **285** and fight the Ogre, but you may deduct 2 points from the Ogre's throw when he rolls for Attack Strength each round. After the fight is over, you must lose the Gold Piece; it is transformed to a useless metal by the spell.

401

Do you have a Goblin's tooth with you? If not, you try in vain to cast the spell and the Elvins are not impressed, tying your hands and kicking you angrily (lose 2 STAMINA points and turn to **218**). If you do have a tooth, you cast your spell over it (deduct 1 STAMINA point) and it forms into a Goblin before their eyes. At first they are apprehensive – they do not like Goblins – but they relax a little as you show them you have complete control over your creation. You can make it dance a jig, stand on its head and even sing (although this causes scores of protests – Goblins have the most tuneless voices imaginable). As a finale, you make it bow down before them and kiss their boots. As the Goblin disappears, the Elvins congratulate you. After a brief chat, they return your backpack and allow you to continue on your way. Turn to **196**.

402

Deduct 1 STAMINA point. You cannot use this spell as you do not have the Green-Haired Wig it requires. As you try to cast it, the beast leaps at you and sinks its teeth into your forearm. Deduct 3 STAMINA points. You must now draw your weapon and fight it – return to 74 and resolve the battle.

403

Deduct 2 STAMINA points. You cast the spell and an expression of pain comes over the Spirit's face. 'Retract that spell!' it screams. 'Or feel the wrath of Mananka!' But its threat is an idle one and the face is disappearing before you. The smoke is quickly collecting together and returning to the box. You are safe. If you have not done so already, you may try the other box (turn to 258). Otherwise you may leave the village (turn to 196).

404

Deduct 1 STAMINA point. You cannot use this spell as you do not have the Sun Jewel it requires. While you are trying in vain to make it work, the Serpent strikes. Lose another 2 STAMINA points. Return to 275 and choose again.

405

Deduct 4 STAMINA points. Flinging your hand forward and casting the spell, a shower of small fireballs burst into the air around the little Elvin. Several of them hit the creature, burning its wings and causing it to drop from the air like a flaming torch. Turn to 121.

406

Deduct 2 STAMINA points. You will now learn an important rule: you cannot cast spells while your hands are bound! You have wasted your efforts. Turn to 112.

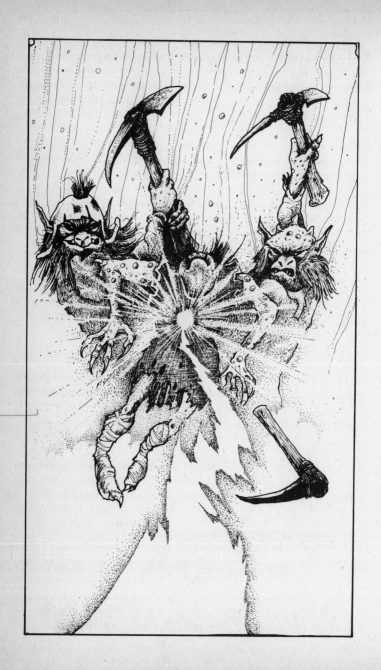

407

Deduct 4 STAMINA points. You cast the spell and point at the first Goblin. A streak of lightning shoots from your finger and catches the creature square in the chest, killing it instantly. The other two stop in their tracks, deciding whether to continue the attack. Roll two dice for each of the remaining Goblins. If the number rolled for either (or both) of them is *equal to or higher than* their SKILL score, this means it will turn and flee into the woods. Otherwise it will continue its attack. Their scores are:

SECOND GOBLIN   SKILL 6   STAMINA 4
THIRD GOBLIN   SKILL 5   STAMINA 5

If you have to fight either of these, and win, turn to **155**. If they both flee, turn to **202**.

408

Deduct 4 STAMINA points. You cast your spell and suddenly the acorn hail ceases. The Elvins look on with wonder as their nuts bounce off an invisible shield. You move smartly onwards until the spell wears off. Turn to **7**.

409

Deduct 2 STAMINA points. You cast the spell at the lock. It begins to hum quietly and little clicks indicate that the tumblers are moving. Eventually it swings apart and you may open the cage. The woman thanks you. She will now reward you for your help. Would you like a magical item (turn to **248**) or an aid in combat (turn to **122**)?

410

Deduct 1 STAMINA point. You fumble with your spell, which does not seem to work. The Wood Golem attacks and smashes you for 2 STAMINA points' worth of damage. You cannot use this spell as you do not have the Gold-Backed Mirror it requires. Return to **87** and choose again.

411

Deduct 2 STAMINA points. You cast the spell and wait. Slowly, the ground moves further from you. You are growing larger! The Hill Giant watches in disbelief while you grow to his size. You may now fight the Giant:

HILL GIANT   SKILL 9   STAMINA 11

But you may double your SKILL while you are under the influence of this spell. If you win, turn to **265**.

412

Deduct 5 STAMINA points. There is no such spell as this. Return to **201** and make another choice.

413

Deduct 5 STAMINA points. There is no such spell as this. Return to **158** and choose again.

414

Deduct 5 STAMINA points. There is no such spell as this. Return to **99** and choose again.

415

Deduct 4 STAMINA points. The creature makes a half turn and swings its deadly tail. But as its sting whips towards you, it hits the invisible force field you have created and does you no damage. Will you now cast an attacking spell (turn to **364**) or draw your weapon and fight it (turn to **227**)?

416

Deduct 5 STAMINA points. There is no such spell as this. Turn to **64**.

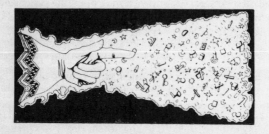

417

Deduct 5 STAMINA points. There is no such spell as this. The snakes are now upon you and are beginning to attack. Roll one die. If you roll 1–5, this is the number of STAMINA points of damage you must sustain. If you roll a 6, the bites are poisonous and you are now spending your last minutes before the poison takes its deadly effect . . . If you have survived, turn back to **63** and choose again.

418

Deduct 5 STAMINA points. You cast your spell but nothing happens. The blast hits you in the chest, killing you instantly. Your journey ends here . . .

419

Deduct 1 STAMINA point. You cast your spell but nothing happens. Will you continue (turn to **73**) or return and take the other path (turn to **51**)?

420

If you do not have enough STAMINA left to cast a spell, you may turn to **227** and fight the creature with your weapon. Otherwise, choose your spell:

ZIP	NIT	FIF	WAL	SUD
347	326	436	447	370

421

Deduct 1 STAMINA point. You cannot use this spell as you do not have the vial of glue you need to cast it. Meanwhile the night creature has attacked and inflicted 2 STAMINA points' worth of damage. Return to **123** and choose again.

422

Deduct 1 STAMINA point. You cannot cast this spell as you do not have the Staff of Oak Sapling it requires. Deduct a further 2 STAMINA points as you try without success to make it work. Then return to **239** and choose again.

423

Deduct 2 STAMINA points. You cast your spell. From somewhere within, a voice speaks to you, telling you to cast the DOP spell to open

the door. This is your only hope unless you are strong enough to break down the door. Return to **66** and choose again.

424

Deduct 2 STAMINA points. You fall down into the pit, but your body moves in the air as if to anticipate your landing. Turn to **277**, where you will be required to make a dice roll. Because of your spell, you may deduct 3 points from the dice roll and you may ignore the extra penalty on a roll of double 6.

425

Do you have any Goblins' teeth with you? If so, you may throw as many as you want on to the floor and cast your spell on them. You must deduct 1 STAMINA point per Goblin you create. Each Goblin will have a SKILL of 5 and a STAMINA of 5 and you may command an attack on the Wolfhound. If your creations kill the beast, turn to **50**; if not, finish it off yourself and turn to **50** if you succeed. If you do not have any Goblins' teeth, then you try in vain to cast the spell and the Wolfhound leaps at your throat, causing you 5 STAMINA points' worth of damage – you will have to fight it:

WOLFHOUND   SKILL 7   STAMINA 6

Turn to **50** if you win.

426

Deduct 2 STAMINA points. The Serpent is ready to attack, but waits for you to move. From within, a feeling of peace comes over you as you look at the creature. You relax a little and the Serpent suddenly disappears once more; but you could swear it *winked* at you before it vanished. It still grips your arm, and pulls you. You decide to continue your journey. Turn to **94**.

427

Deduct 5 STAMINA points. There is no such spell as this. Return to **166** and choose again.

428

Deduct 5 STAMINA points. There is no such spell as this. The Goblins are quickly on you and attack you for 2 STAMINA points' worth of damage. You may, if you wish, *Test your Luck* and if you are Lucky you avoid this attack. Return to **217** and fight them or cast another spell.

429

Deduct 1 STAMINA point. You cannot use this spell as you do not have the Potion of Fire Water it requires. Return to **4** and choose again.

430

Deduct 5 STAMINA points. There is no such spell as this. Turn to **256**.

431

Deduct 4 STAMINA points. You cast the spell and a protective force-field surrounds your body. You may turn to **79**, but no harm will befall you as there will be no contact between you and any of the villagers.

432

Deduct 5 STAMINA points. There is no such spell as this. While you are reciting it, the Troll springs at you, and a lucky blow knocks you to the floor. Before you can rise, the creature is on you, sinking its slimy teeth into your throat. Your journey has ended here . . .

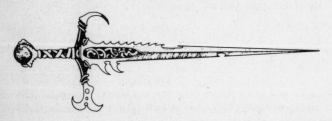

433

Deduct 4 STAMINA points. You cast the spell and, commanding the snakes, they back away from you. For the present, you are safe. But how may you escape from the pit? If you have not yet called on help from Libra, turn to **273**. But if you have already used her help, there is little you can do but hold the snakes off until your STAMINA runs out – your journey has ended here . . .

434

Deduct 1 STAMINA point. You cast the spell but nothing happens. You panic, but there is little you can do to avoid the deadly blast. Your journey is over . . .

435

Deduct 5 STAMINA points. You cast your spell, but nothing happens. Will you continue (turn to 73) or return and take the other path (turn to 51)?

436

Deduct 5 STAMINA points. There is no such spell as this. Turn to 307.

437

Deduct 5 STAMINA points. There is no such spell as this. Return to 123 and choose again.

438

Deduct 4 STAMINA points. You cast the spell and a bolt of lightning shoots from your fingertip at the creature, hitting it square in the chest. It reels and falls backwards, dead, on to the floor. Turn to 186.

439

Deduct 5 STAMINA points. There is no such spell as this. You fall down into the pit. Turn to 277.

440

Deduct 5 STAMINA points. There is no such spell as this. Return to 74 and choose again.

441

Deduct 1 STAMINA point. Do you have a Gold Piece with you? If not, the spell does not work and the little Elvin zips down and cuts you again for 2 STAMINA points' worth of damage (return to 203 and choose again). If you have a coin, you place it on your wrist and cast the spell. An invisible shield forms around your forearm, and you may use this in defence. Return to 203 and fight the Elvin, but because of your shield you may deduct 2 points from the Elvin's dice roll for Attack Strength each round. After the fight, the Gold Piece is no longer usable.

442

Deduct 1 STAMINA point and cast your spell. Do you have any beeswax with you? If so, you have rubbed it on your sword and it now has been magically enhanced. Return to 217 and fight the Goblins but, each time you hit a Goblin, you may double the damage you do. If you do not have beeswax, you *believe* your weapon has been sharpened, but it has not and will do only normal damage. If you have used this spell successfully before, you have now used all your beeswax. Otherwise you have used half your original portion.

443

Deduct 5 STAMINA points. There is no such spell as this. Return to 4 and choose again.

444

Deduct 5 STAMINA points. There is no such spell as this. Return to 201 and choose again.

445

Deduct 5 STAMINA points. There is no such spell as this. Turn to 64.

446

Deduct 5 STAMINA points. Unfortunately, there is no such spell as this and the time you have wasted on casting it leaves you no time to plan another escape. The boulder crushes you. Your journey has ended here . . .

447

Deduct 4 STAMINA points. The Manticore is in the opposite passage preparing to pounce at you. You cast your spell as it leaps and it roars loudly as it hits your invisible wall in mid-flight! Using your control, you fence it in securely, allowing you to grab the Svinn girl and run from the cave. Turn to 456.

448

Deduct 4 STAMINA points. The creature stops in its tracks and you order it to return to the woods from where it came. Having escaped the creature you may return to your original reference.

449

Deduct 2 STAMINA points. You wait for the spell to take effect and you begin to hear a voice from within. The mysterious voice is telling you that your safest bet is to avoid this door and leave the mine. If you take heed of this warning, turn to 144. If you wish to continue trying the door, turn to 268 and choose again.

450

Deduct 1 STAMINA point. You cannot cast this spell as you do not have the Bracelet of Bone it requires. In actual fact, you cannot cast *any* spell when your hands are bound (remember this in future). Turn to 112.

451

Deduct 5 STAMINA points. You cast the spell but nothing happens. Return to 220 and choose again.

452

Deduct 1 STAMINA point. You cast your spell but nothing happens. Return to 117 and choose again.

453

Deduct 2 STAMINA points. You cast the spell and begin to grow to three times your normal size. The night creature stops in its tracks. You may, if you wish, *Test your Luck*. If you are Lucky, the beast takes flight and runs back into the woods. If you are Unlucky, or if you did not *Test your Luck*, the creature continues to attack but you may double your SKILL score as you attack it. Return to 123.

454

Deduct 2 STAMINA points. You cast this spell and consider both directions. Inside your mind, you begin to feel differently when you face through the door and when you face back into the room. Looking through the door, a hot sweat comes over your face, and looking back into the room at your entrance door, this feeling subsides and you feel calm. Will you press on ahead through the door (turn to 6) or retrace your steps through the room (turn to 120)?

455

Deduct 2 STAMINA points. You cast the spell and a darkness descends over the room. The Spirit calls out to you, 'You cannot escape from me, mortal!' But under the cover of darkness, you have slipped out of the hut. You leave the village. Turn to 196.

You leave the Manticore's chamber and follow the path to the source of the light. As you had hoped, a cave entrance allows you out on to the side of the hill. You and the Svinn girl find your way back to Torrepani. The Svinn chief is overjoyed to have his daughter back and the village erupts into celebration as their curse is now lifted. You are given the freedom of the village and decide to stay for the day to recuperate. You visit the Svinn healing-priest who will treat your wounds, cure any diseases and lift curses which you may have. Restore your SKILL, STAMINA and LUCK points to their *Initial* values. The priest may also rid you of the annoying little Minimite if he is still with you.

You sleep heavily that night and rise the next morning to continue on your way. Before you go, the Svinn chief meets you. He hands you two gifts: a pouch containing 10 Gold Pieces and a large key. 'I know you head for Kharé,' says the chief, 'but the city is evil and you must be on your guard. Two years ago a traveller passed through here from Kharé and gave me this key, saying he would never return. This is a key to the city gates and with it you will be able to enter the city unnoticed.' Once you get to Kharé's south gate, in the next adventure, you may turn to **12** if you wish to use this key.

You thank him and leave Torrepani. You have made friends here and may permanently increase your *Initial* LUCK score by 1 point. Soon the path is leading you on from the Shamutanti Hills down across rice fields towards a great walled city – the Cityport of Kharé – and on to the next stage of your quest . . .